Helion & Company Limited
Unit 8 Amherst Business Centre
Budbrooke Road
Warwick
CV34 5WE
England
Tel. 01926 499 619
Fax 0121 711 4075
Email: info@helion.co.uk
Website: www.helion.co.uk
Twitter: @helionbooks
Visit our blog http://blog.helion.co.uk/

Published by Helion & Company 2019
Designed and typeset by Farr out Publications, Wokingham, Berkshire
Cover designed by Paul Hewitt, Battlefield Design (www.battlefield-design.co.uk)
Printed by Henry Ling Limited, Dorchester, Dorset

ISBN 978-1-911628-70-5

British Library Cataloguing-in-Publication Data
A catalogue record for this book is available from the British Library

We always welcome receiving book proposals from prospective authors.

CONTENTS

ABBREVIATIONS

ASW	anti-submarine warfare
COAN	*Comando de la Aviación Naval Argentina* (Argentine Naval Aviation)
CERTSUB	certain submarine (target classification)
ECM	electronic countermeasures
ESM	electronic support measures
MAD	magnetic anomaly detector
POSSUB	possible submarine
PROBSUB	probable submarine
TF	task force

AUTHOR'S NOTES

This book is not about the entire history of the conflict over the Falklands/Malvinas Islands in 1982, but just about a very small part of it. Much has been written about this war and thus the story in question is limited to that once Argentina 'recovered' or 'invaded' (depending on from which side of the fence one looks at it) the islands on the 2 April of that year. The United Kingdom then sent a huge Task Force, the largest it had put together since the Second World War. The bloody conflict ended seventy-four days later, when the Union Jack was raised once again in the capital of the islands. The sovereignty dispute over the Falklands/Malvinas remains unresolved to this day. However, the topic of sovereignty is not further discussed in this book. To avoid any discussion (and along UN guidelines) about the names of the islands and or their locations, their names in English and Spanish are used. Locations and geographic features on continental Argentina are named in Spanish only: *golfo* is gulf, *cabo* is cape, *bahía* is bay, and *isla* is isle.

For better understanding of ranks used by the two navies, and while observing that those cited in the book are as at the time of the events, the following table is a list of their equivalents for the *Armada Argentina* (left column) and the Royal Navy (right column).

As far as the vocabulary is concerned, some technical terms have been used where necessary and hopefully it is not too difficult to follow for the average reader. Likewise, we have tried to minimise the use of acronyms and abbreviations. An anti-submarine warfare (ASW) specialist will know how to forgive me.

Finally, all times cited are local time or GMT+3.

Oficiales	**Officers**	***Suboficiales***	**Ratings**
Almirante	Admiral	*Suboficial Mayor*	Warrant Officer
Vicealmirante	Vice Admiral	*Suboficial Principal*	Warrant Officer
Contralmirante	Rear Admiral	*Suboficial Primero*	Chief Petty Officer
Comodoro de Marina	Commodore	*Suboficial Segundo*	Petty Officer
Capitán de Navío	Captain	*Cabo Principal*	Leading Hand
Capitán de Fragata	Commander	*Cabo Primero*	Leading Hand
Capitán de Corbeta	Lieutenant-Commander	*Cabo Segundo*	Able Seaman 1
Teniente de Navío	Lieutenant	*Marinero Primero*	Able Seaman 2
Teniente de Fragata	Sub-Lieutenant	*Marinero Segundo*	New Entry
Teniente de Corbeta	Acting Sub-Lieutenant		
Guardiamarina	Acting Sub-Lieutenant		

FOREWORD

In 1982, during the Falklands/Malvinas War, the United Kingdom sent five of its most modern nuclear-powered submarines, and at least one diesel-electric or conventional submarine, to the South Atlantic. At the time, the Argentine Navy possessed little knowledge of the operational capabilities or technical characteristics of these nuclear-powered boats. The dramatic sinking of the Argentine Cruiser *General Belgrano* made it absolutely clear that the self-protection measures employed by the surface units of the Argentine fleet, though appropriate, were going to be insufficient.

Over the years, and with more information about the actions of the British submarines coming to light, it is now possible to appreciate how the deployment and concentration of these nuclear-powered submarines in the hunt for surface units was of proportions never seen before in any theatre of war. The scope of the underwater operations of these non-conventional units was helped by their relatively high speed and their almost infinite range of action, together with the discretion and autonomy that their method of propulsion granted them. In addition, the use of satellites facilitated an enormous capacity for command and the distribution of orders, and the control of naval units deployed in remote and distant parts of the globe.

Mariano Sciaroni has presented a vibrant and lucid account of the actions of both sides in this war. Having carried out a thorough investigation, accessing documents never previously available, he presents in his own enjoyable and educational style, descriptions of the technologies, equipment and processes employed, alongside the knowledge and spirit of the men who used them.

I am sure that the reader will find an intelligent compilation of technical information in this book along with a historical and strategic appreciation of previously unknown aspects of this part of the war at sea, and many enlightening and vibrant stories from the protagonists of the action during those days.

We have here a splendid and at times emotive story of the actions of the submariners and submarine hunters of the last war at sea. It is for this reason that I consider it to be an important contribution to the yet unexplained aspects of the war that any interested reader would surely appreciate and value.

Héctor Alfredo Skare
Capitán de Navío VGM (Retired), Naval Aviator
Commander Task Unit 80.2.2, "Malvinas War"
Argentine Navy "Maritime Recon and
Antisubmarine Warfare" air unit.

INTRODUCTION

The first time I heard something about the role of the Argentine Navy during the Falklands/Malvinas War was at the end of the last century. During the last few months of my time at university, several friends from the students' organisation had taken it upon themselves to organise a seminar about the Falklands/Malvinas War, to which they invited *Almirante* Enrique E. Molina Pico who at that time was the Argentine Navy's Chief of Staff.

At first, I was surprised to hear about the large number of nautical miles that he sailed during the war in command of a destroyer, especially those carried out as an escort to the aircraft carrier. As with many people outside the Navy, I had a false impression that immediately after the sinking of the *Belgrano*, the remaining ships of the fleet had rapidly sought sanctuary in port.

My second surprise came a couple of years later when I read accounts on the internet regarding the anti-submarine operations that took place on 5 May. Not only had the Argentine Fleet not immediately entered port, but it had also attacked submerged contacts. I was astounded.

Unfortunately, I heard nothing else about the subject over the next few years. It seemed that the protagonists considered that nothing about it was worth telling – that was until I came across and article in the Central Naval Bulletin, written by *Capitán de Fragata* (R) Enrique Fortini (or "Quique") in which he told the story of these forgotten actions carried out from the aircraft carrier ARA *25 de Mayo*.

The war carried out against submarines is, without doubt, less spectacular than that of explosion and missiles being launched by fast combat jets. It's an exercise in patience carried out by analysing a console, located either in the fuselage of a slow-moving propeller driven aircraft or helicopter, or in the bowels of a ship, attempting to decipher whether a noise being listened to is from submarine or a whale, or even a submerged volcano. It's as fascinating as it sounds.

Maybe, as I had always preferred "The Hunt for Red October" over "Top Gun", combined with the details contained in Fortini´s excellent account, I became motivated to add my own grain of sand to the history of the conflict. This consisted of a short essay in which I ended by concluding that it seemed probable that an unidentified British submarine had been attacked by the Argentine naval forces in those days of May 1982.

A few months after the publication of the article, I received some emails from two naval officers, "Quique" Fortini being one of them, and from this began a friendly email exchange about antisubmarine warfare. During the exchange of emails between us, Enrique suggested that we should write something concise about the anti-submarine war in the Falklands/Malvinas, and over time we began to discuss first a longer article, then a small book and finally we began to dream of a book that would completely cover the subject – a definitive work about the anti-submarine war, focused on the first days in May in the South Atlantic.

The book would obviously be centred on the Anti-Submarine Naval Air Squadron as it was its personnel who had achieved the most contacts and attacks that had taken place. The rest of the participants, from the Sea Kings to the destroyers, had had a smaller role in the events than the 'owls'.

Obviously, we believed that most veterans would be keen to share their stories from the time of the conflict (an anti-submarine mission is a combat mission after all), but apart from a fervent nucleus, we did not get nearly as many accounts as we had expected.

We were also surprised by the Royal Navy. Initially we were convinced that the old foe would never agree to our request to access the war diaries of the nuclear submarines. In fact, we didn't even expect to get a response, bearing in mind the only precedent that we were aware of was of a British Parliamentarian that had requested access to these documents, without success.

However, after a long battle and walking of the legal route (in other words, we didn't ask for but demanded access to the public information based on the United Kingdom's Freedom of Information laws) we finally obtained copies of Reports of Proceedings from submarines HMS *Spartan* and HMS *Splendid*.

It was on that January day that we started to complete the full story of the events, now that we could begin to match up the story of what had happened on the surface with that which had taken place below. Later, HMS *Conqueror's* and HMS *Valiant's* Report of Proceedings arrived, and we could complete the circle.

Amongst other things, we discovered the mission flown on 4 May by *Teniente de Navío* Juan José Membrana, which would appear to have been nothing unusual from the point of view of the submarine hunters, had greatly surprised the crew of HMS *Splendid*. It was also clear that the crew of the Fokker of the Argentine Air Force had, in fact, not been talking nonsense when they had claimed to have seen a submarine on 6 May.

However, the most interesting thing was the confirmation that no British submarine had been attacked on 5 May 1982 by the Naval Aviation, which pulled the rug from under all theories written about it up until then.

Of course, this makes us wonder which country this submarine had been from? The contact had submarine masts, made the noise of a submarine and behaved like a submarine. In other words, if it has four legs and barks, it is a dog. The same in this case, but under water.

It is worth pointing out that other documents were not released to us, but this was always justified with the reason for this rejection. In short, the British bureaucratic system complied with the prescribed laws and within the time required. We also found some other interesting articles, conference interviews and books, none of them well known, which contained some surprising revelations, such as a British submarine had been snooping around the approaches to Buenos Aires in April 1982.

Using the information that we had obtained, we believed that we had managed to get close to the limit of public knowledge about the attacks carried out by the Argentine Navy on submarines during the war. We pushed as far as we could the sources of information available to us. We hope that this book will be the beginning, not the end, of the debate about what happened under the waters of the South Atlantic. With that end in mind and with the hope that someone beyond the seas picks up the glove, it is aggressive and polemic in some places.

Finally, and putting forward somewhat our conclusions, it is worth saying that it is our conviction that the Argentine Navy achieved a lot in the anti-submarine war, giving rise to improvisations and at the same time suffering from the negligence carried over from years before. The fact that the British did not manage to sink the aircraft carrier was simple; because they could not.

I must make clear the real drive behind all of this has been the late *Capitán de Fragata* (Retired) Enrique Fortini. It was him that gave the push to start this, organised the interviews and gave his help on all fronts, correcting various pages and he who paid for the coffees during our meetings. But I am the only person responsible, from both a literary and historical standpoint: any mistakes, therefore, are only mine.

I do not want to end this introduction without making the pertinent acknowledgments. First, I'd like to thank all who have given me hours of their time to relive forgotten moments as well as those who have participated but have not wanted – for various reasons – to reveal their names.

I have also used many sources for obtaining information used in this book. Therefore, I need to express my gratitude to the personnel from the Argentine Navy Archive, to the management of the department of Historical Studies of the Argentine Air Force, and its director *Comodoro* (R) Oscar Aranda Durañona, Alejandro Amendolara, Pablo Castro, Mike Demetriou from the FOIA Office, George Malcolmson (Archivist at the Royal Navy Submarine Museum) and countless other people from various government offices in Argentina, the UK and USA.

My special gratitude is due to Andy Smith, who kindly translated the original Spanish manuscript of this book.

Finally, this work is dedicated to my family, my wife Natasha and my children: Lola, Tomás and Lucas.

1
BANZAI NIGHT

> Lieutenant Commander Ono, the Staff Intelligence Officer, quickly plotted the enemy's reported position on the navigation chart and measured off the distance between it and our force. The enemy was just 200 miles away! This meant that he was already within striking range of our planes, but if he had carriers, we were also within his reach. (*Midway, The Battle That Doomed Japan, the Japanese Navy's Story*, by Mitsuo Fuchida and Masatake Okumiya).

Under any other circumstances, it would have been a good day for sailing, contemplating the sunset from the flight deck while smoking a cigarette.

However, the anxiety of the sailors and aviators on board the Argentine Navy's ships that were scouring the South Atlantic in search of the opposing fleet, was slowly increasing. They were the last hours of Labour Day (1 May 1982), and Task Force 79 (probably denominated in this way in honour of course number 79 of the Naval Military School, to which most of the skippers of the naval units had belonged) was preparing itself under the orders of its commander, *Contralmirante* Gualter O. Allara, to deliver an initial "massive attack against enemy units".

His superior, Chief of Naval Operations *Vicealmirante* Juan José Lombardo was convinced that the enemy's units were carrying out an amphibious operation on the shores of the Falklands/Malvinas Islands.

The latest action in the war in the islands had already begun a few hours before. The Royal Air Force had dropped a stick of bombs across the runway of Port Stanley (Puerto Argentino) from the belly of a Vulcan bomber based on Ascension Island. Soon after, Sea Harrier jets, launched from the British aircraft carriers, had attacked the Argentine defences. On the islands it was all chaos and adrenaline and reports of amphibious and helicopter landings were increasing exponentially.

This was deemed to be the decisive moment to act and bloody the nose of the "British invaders" by means of a classic aeronaval action. However, it was necessary to take advantage of the factor of surprise as this would be the only way to overcome and neutralise the numerical and technological advantages the Royal Navy possessed.

Before this could happen, however, it was necessary to get an up to date position of the British fleet. To this end, the fleet commander requested that the versatile Anti-Submarine Naval Air Squadron take off once again with its Tracker aircraft.

ARA *25 de Mayo* in the South Atlantic, before the 1982 conflict. Five Skyhawks, an Alouette and two Sea King helicopters are visible on the flight deck. (*Armada Argentina*)

It was another dangerous reconnaissance mission, well within reach of the Sea Harrier fighter aircraft and their lethal AIM-9L Sidewinder air-to-air missiles. It was not the first search mission for the Trackers to carry out that day. Earlier, at 1513 hrs, they had located part of the hostile force at 031° off Port Stanley (or Puerto Argentino) and 120 nautical miles away. This enemy task force, consisting of the aircraft carriers and their escorts, was protecting the forces engaged in the alleged (and in reality, non-existent) amphibious action.

An enemy aircraft carrier would be a juicy target. Without their carriers, the amphibious fleet would not have any air cover, and without that, any sane admiral would refrain from carrying out a landing on the islands.

The attack was organised for first light of the following day, an attack that would attempt to redirect the course of events through a "Battle of Midway" in the South Atlantic.

The initial move would be an attack by the A-4Q Skyhawk fighter-bombers of the Third Fighter and Attack Naval Air Squadron (*Tercera Escuadrilla Aeronaval de Caza y Ataque*), which would take advantage of the element of surprise and attack the enemy force with bombs.

The commander of the squadron, *Capitán de Corbeta* Rodolfo Castro Fox remembers:

> Six A-4Qs were prepared for action, each armed with four Mk 82 bombs. I was to lead the attack and a further aircraft would be readied in reserve and another to act as a tanker for the return. By using the table of probabilities, considering the capability of the British anti-aircraft defences, of our six-initial aircraft, four would get into a position to drop their bombs and only two would make it back.
>
> Of the 16 bombs that we would release, there would be a probability of impact of 25 percent, in other words, four bombs of 500 pounds. This could neutralise an aircraft carrier and the loss of four aircraft would be acceptable.

Later, in line with the plan of attack, the aeronaval blow and the confusion amongst the British ships would be exploited by the three A-69 class corvettes (ARA *Drummond*, *Guerrico* and *Granville*) which would fire a salvo of Exocet MM-38 anti-ship missiles at any British ship that had remained afloat.

The big advantage the corvettes possessed was their small size, which meant that they would only appear on the enemy radar screens when they were at around 20 nautical miles distance from the British ships, while the British ships would appear on their French Thomson-CSF radar at much greater distances. This would mean that they would have the advantage of being able to shoot first and even escape before any counterattack.

For this bold operation, the Task Forces were organised as follows:

- **TG 79.1**: Aircraft Carrier ARA *25 de Mayo*, Destroyers ARA *Santísima Trinidad*, ARA *Hércules* and ARA *Py*; oiler YPF *Campo Durán*.
- **TG 79.4**: Corvettes ARA *Drummond*, ARA *Guerrico* and ARA *Granville*; oiler *Punta Médanos*.

For the *coup de grâce* following the northern part of the pincer attack, a task force centred on the cruiser ARA *General Belgrano* would arrive from the south, causing an additional problem for the British forces. This was composed of:

- **TG 79.3**: Cruiser ARA *General Belgrano* and its escort destroyers ARA *Bouchard* and ARA *Piedrabuena* (the oiler that had been

The ground crew loading A-4Q Skyhawk 3-A-305 with 500-lb Snakeye bombs for the early May attack against the British Task Force. *Capitán de Corbeta* Rodolfo Castro Fox, the unit's commander, is in the extreme right of the picture. (*Armada Argentina*)

ARA *Guerrico*, a French made A-69 or *D'Estienne d'Orves* Class corvette, pictured at South Georgia on 3 April 1982. (*Armada Argentina*)

A port bow view of the Argentine aircraft carrier ARA *25 de Mayo* in port during exercise UNITAS XX. (US Navy)

supporting them had already left the formation).

According to the cruiser's commander, the late *Capitán de Navío* Héctor Bonzo:

> The aircraft carrier *25 de Mayo* was part of a Task Force that was going to approach the area around the Malvinas from the north. Meanwhile the *Belgrano*, along with two destroyers, would advance from the south as part of a pincer movement on the British ships.

To everyone it was clear that the success of the operation depended on the professionalism and luck of the naval aviators (possibly in this order). They were the tip of the spear, and it was hoped that they would be sufficiently sharp.

Deep within the bowels of *25 de Mayo* (or the POMA according to its administrative designation in the Argentine Navy) some faces were beginning to show the weight of responsibility and anguish. They were beginning to prepare the weapons for what the naval aviators would call the 'Banzai Night', after the war cry of Japanese suicide pilots. As then *Capitán de Fragata* Bernardo Viglierchio, Operations Officer on board *25 de Mayo* during those days of May – and therefore in charge of the aero naval attack organisation later recalled:

> I had an existential crisis, the angst that I was suffering was unspeakable. I was conscious that I was practically sending the pilots that would fly the mission to their deaths.

Without doubt another hand stroking a bulkhead, and a mind full of ideas would think that in a few hours, if things went to plan, a bomb would impact a similar bulkhead on an enemy ship. However, if everything went exceedingly badly, possibly it would be *25 de Mayo* that would be damaged or even sunk. That thought was perturbing. Nobody would dare touch our aircraft carrier!

The elderly V-2 ARA *25 de Mayo*, which had a displacement of 15,892 tonnes and a crew of more than 1,500, was British-built and

An A-4Q on the deck of ARA *25 de Mayo* during a post-war exercise. Note the new paint scheme on some aircraft. (*Armada Argentina*)

had originally been launched as HMS *Venerable*.

Launched in 1943, she had made a name for herself supporting the allied efforts in the Pacific Theatre during the last stages of the Second World War. She was incorporated into the Argentine Navy in 1969, having first passed through the hands of the Dutch Navy from 1948 where it was operated with the name of HMNLS *Karel Doorman*.

It was a rather ironic twist of fate that, in May 1982, she was being pitted against her original constructors. Of course, this was not the same ship that had been delivered by the shipyards of the United Kingdom. During her operational life she had undergone a series of modernisations. The first of these had been in 1955, when the straight flight deck had been modified to an angled one (8° with respect to the ship). Also, among other modifications, a single steam catapult was added to the bow; the electronics were improved; and the aircraft-lifts and island were redesigned. Such modifications were typical of the period for aircraft carriers which had been constructed only with the thought of operating piston engined aircraft and now needed to be updated to enter the jet age era.

The second of the important refits which the ship had took place in Argentina between 1980 and 1981, and included reinforcing the flight deck and making other changes necessary to be able to operate the Dassault-Breguet Super Etendard fighter-bombers that were in the process of being introduced into service. However, during the conflict that took place in the South Atlantic its Carrier Air Wing only consisted of Douglas A-4Q Skyhawks; Grumman S-2E Tracker anti-submarine aircraft; Sikorsky SH-3D Sea King heavy helicopters and Aérospatiale Alouette III light helicopters.

The condition of the ship could be described as adequate for its role (especially the electronics and communications equipment), with the exception of its propulsion system which, in short, reduced the operational capability of the ship. As better described by *Capitán* Viglierchio:

> The condition of the ship was adequate, when considering that it was 30-something years old. In this case it was a ship constructed by the British, modified by the Dutch and then operated by the Argentine Navy. In 1976, a list had been drawn up of the necessary and important tasks that needed to be carried out to improve its general condition. Some of these had been carried out and others were in the process of being done – but for all this the propulsion system continued to be of 1945 vintage with a boiler damaged and repaired in 1964. This was the most deficient system in the ship and it seriously limited its operational capability, with only a reduced maximum navigation speed being possible.

There was also ample experience within the Argentine Navy of the operation of this aircraft carrier. At least the crew was sufficiently well trained for the task. *Capitán* Viglierchio added:

> In 1982 between the months of January and February, as was usual, personnel transfers were carried out and the training of the new crew commenced. This training was carried at different levels, depending on elements such as the percentage of new postings in each department and the level of knowledge and previous experience of those newly posted. That is to say that, at the beginning of the year, different levels of training were carried out (individually and in each operational group).
>
> In 1982 the Operations Officer, Wings and Comms Officer had a good level of experience (in my case, I had been Flight Deck Officer and Wings and had had seven years on board as part of the embarked squadrons). At the same time, it is important to mention that the Commander of the ship, *Capitán* Sarcona, had repeated his

ARA *25 de Mayo.* (*Armada Argentina*)

command of 1981, which was decisive for the complex and sudden start of real operations. Finally, related to the training of the crew, at the end of the first cruise at sea (March 1982) a sufficient level of proficiency had been obtained, in line with the usual requirements for that time of year. Obviously, had we known what lay in front of us, we would have been a little more demanding!

Overall the ship was at a good operation level in conjunction with experience in her use and a crew that had been well trained. Her only deficiency was the lack of speed. This would have a large impact later, which could not have been foreseen.

On her combat cruise, the aircraft carrier was not alone and unprotected, but was escorted by several ships which augmented the combat capability of the Task Force.

The *25 de Mayo* was being accompanied by two Type 42 destroyers: ARA *Santísima Trinidad* and ARA *Hércules*. In addition, the older destroyer ARA *Py*, an old sea wolf dating from the Second World War, provided the main surface protection of the group against the underwater threat, since it had an excellent sonar equipment.

Tactically, as noted in the carrier's log at 2110 hrs, *25 de Mayo* was sailing at the centre of the formation with *Py* in front of it and the two "42s" on either side, with a separation of four nautical miles between each of them. The formation was completed by the oiler *Campo Durán*, which supported the ships with the resupply of fuel, something that was completely necessary due to the thirsty warship engines.

The attack planned to take place in the first hours of the following day did, in fact, not come to fruition. Uncommonly, on that now seemingly distant afternoon of the 1st May, the wind that usually ravaged the seas in this area stopped blowing. This meant that the A-4Q fighter-bombers could not be launched without significantly reducing the weight of the load they carried.

The problem was that the aircraft needed an amount of wind relative to the flight deck to enable them to be launched with their full load of bombs. However, there was not enough wind (and not enough speed from the *25 de Mayo*) and according to the Navy meteorologists, these conditions would persist for some more hours. Bearing in mind the projected losses from interception and anti-aircraft fire, it was decided that the mission was not going to be worth the risk if the Skyhawks were launched with a lighter bomb load, which is to say, the loss of so many aircraft and pilots to arrive at the target with such a light load was considered not acceptable.

Teniente de Navío Carlos Cal, a pilot embarked on the aircraft carrier, remembered the strange quirk of nature:

Photo taken from Type 42 destroyer ARA *Santísima Trinidad* as it escorted aircraft carrier ARA *25 de Mayo.* (via Enrique Fortini)

> There was a period of some 12 hours in which we could have mounted a surprise attack, but unfortunately the A-4 attack aircraft that operated from *25 de Mayo* needed wind, but it was completely calm. I always maintain that this day could have been the Midway of the South Atlantic. However, unfortunately, nature did not collaborate with us but with the British forces.

Also, *Capitán* Viglierchio expressed:

> That day, in that position, there was a phenomenon that the Argentine sailors could not believe. In the South Atlantic there was absolutely no wind, something that the meteorologists were predicting would last for at least twenty-four hours. Over the period of the afternoon and evening a series of changes to the configuration of the A-4s took place. From the original load of four bombs each, this was reduced to three and then later two which would have made the attack not very effective.

For this reason, the projected mission due to take place in the early hours the following day did not take place.

Besides the lack of wind, at 0030 hrs on the 2nd May, the element of surprise was definitively lost when *25 de Mayo* was located by the enemy: Sea Harrier aircraft that had been following Tracker 2-AS-26 (one of the planes launched to locate the enemy fleet) had been illuminated by 965 radar (air search) and then by 909 radar (fire control radar for Sea Dart missile) by one of the two Type 42 destroyers which, it was assumed, gave away the position of the Argentine fleet.

According to *Capitán* José Luís Tejo, commander of ARA *Santísima*

Type 42 destroyer ARA *Hércules.* (*Armada Argentina*)

Trinidad:

> We gained a lock with the 909 radar on a contact 40 miles from our own forces. Both Harriers immediately stopped their approach and retreated. The decision to take this step was mine...but not to save the Tracker, which was not really in any danger as it was already some way ahead of the Harriers (approximately 15-20 miles)...I took the decision as protection measure for the Task Force, for which I was responsible, with the aim of getting the Harriers to stop their approach, no doubt already alerted by their passive sensors that they had been illuminated by missile control radars; or in the case that they had continued towards us, to have them locked up once they were within range of our Sea Dart missiles, allowing us to shoot them down at the maximum range with the possibility of firing a second missile should the first one not hit the target. This action, in which we were followed by *Hércules* and its 909 radars, was successful because the aircraft went away.

The British version of events is slightly different. In theory, they had the vague notion of the position of the aircraft carrier, having already received this information from an electronic reconnaissance satellite belonging to the United States (a "White Cloud" satellite), which had detected the characteristic electronic emissions from the radar of one of the escorts.

With this information, they sent a single Sea Harrier to try to locate the Argentine fleet. Although the two versions of events don't match, they both agree on the fundamental point that the British fixed the position of the aircraft carrier and its escorts.

The only aircraft that finally located the fleet belonged to 801 Naval Air Squadron of the Royal Navy, and was being flown by Flight Lieutenant Ian "Morts" Mortimer, who would later be shot down on 1 June over Port Stanley (Puerto Argentino) by the Roland anti-aircraft missile system of the Argentine Army.

The then Commander Nigel Ward, in charge of the squadron, later wrote about the incident and the post-flight debriefing of his subordinate which revealed the British version of events:

> I went out high-level, as briefed, Boss; radar silent. Let down at 200 miles and covered the next 40 miles at 200 feet. There wasn't a sound from the radar warner and not a light to be seen anywhere. At that point, I thought we had got it wrong. Then I switched my radar to transmit and, as we expected it might, all hell broke loose! The next thing I knew I was being illuminated by all sorts of radar including Sea Dart fire-control, and I counted four ship contacts less than 25 miles away. They obviously had at least one Type 42 out there.
>
> What did you do?
>
> Morts gave me that old-fashioned look and then laughed – with feeling.
>
> I switched off the radar and fucked off, Boss! (Ward, *Sea Harrier over the Falklands*)

Concluding that the planned attack was not possible, and their fleet had been located by the enemy (thus completely losing the element of surprise), the commander of the Argentine Task Force informed his superiors in the mainland, at 0145 hrs, that they would momentarily withdraw from the area of operations.

He immediately ordered the aircraft carrier and its escorts to head away on a course of 230° in the direction of Puerto Deseado and to stay above the 48° south latitude. Heading to the waters close to the continent, where the depth was shallow, would limit the effectiveness of whichever enemy submarine might be sent after them, which was the main worry from this point for the Argentine fleet. As if that were not enough, another Tracker flight on the morning of 2 May confirmed the Task Force had also retreated, frustrating any possibility of mounting an attack even with a reduced bomb load.

On the morning of 2 May there was a fundamental change in tactics of the Argentine Fleet. At this moment, its main aim stopped being to organise a massive attack (both air and/or surface) against the British task force and became to counter the threat of the enemy force. From being an offensive fleet, it became one that was on the defensive.

Of course, the main threat for the Argentine naval forces was represented by the nuclear-powered attack submarines, as much for

Torpedo attack! US Navy carrier USS *Wasp* burning after being hit by three torpedoes launched from a Japanese submarine in the South Pacific, on 15 September 1942. The ship was a total loss. (US Navy)

their ability to travel almost permanently submerged as for their capability of reaching and maintaining high speeds (usually around 30 knots in deep waters), which allowed them to choose when, where and how to carry out torpedo attacks. It is therefore easy to understand that the commander of the TG 79.1 could foresee that the flagship would be the key objective for the British submarines.

Both Prime Minister Thatcher and Admiral Woodward, the latter being in command of the British Carrier Battle Group (Task Force 317.8), found themselves particularly worried about *25 de Mayo*.

The fact was, over-evaluating the true capacity of the Carrier Air Wing, the British intelligence services had believed, albeit incorrectly, that the new Super Etendard attack aircraft, which had been recently acquired from the French, along with a batch of AM-39 Exocet missiles, were able to operate from the aircraft carrier. What worried the Royal Navy was that this would have given the Carrier Air Wing the ability to attack targets effectively "beyond the horizon", something that finally happened on 4 May when HMS *Sheffield* was impacted by this type of missile.

In fact, such was the concern that as early as 23 April the commander of the nuclear attack submarine HMS *Splendid,* had had the carrier in view through his periscope. However, he was unable to commence an attack due to the Rules of Engagement then in force[1]. These would not allow, at this time, any attack on Argentine vessels outside the exclusion zone – the area included within a 200-mile radius circle centred on the islands. However, by 2 May these had changed.

On the afternoon of 30 April, following some days of arduous discussions, the British War Cabinet had specifically authorised the sinking of the aircraft carrier outside the Total Exclusion Zone, which had come into force that same day, without any prior provocation (unless it was located within the Argentine territorial waters or located north of 35° or west of 48°)[2]. To carry out the task of sinking the aircraft carrier, both *Splendid* and *Spartan* (another nuclear submarine) were patrolling to the north of the islands.

Besides their modern and sensitive sonar, the submarines also relied upon the invaluable help of satellites and up to date intelligence based on the interception of communications of the Argentine Navy. So much so that, a few hours after the decision was taken to attack the movement-limited Task Force (because it was protecting the amphibious assault, the Argentine Navy supposed), the following intelligence signal arrived at the British Task Force:

> It is believed that a major Argentine attack is planned for 2 May. BELGRANO is deploying to a position 54.00S 060.00W to attack targets of opportunity S of the Falkland Islands. The CVA group is believed to be deploying into the TEZ during darkness to launch air attacks against British Task Force at first light. A Task Force of 3× A69 frigates and PUNTA MENDANOS deploying to attack any dispersed units of Task Force.

The entire Argentine Navy Battle plan! Fortunately, due to the very general position of the ships supplied by the British intelligence services, the Argentine Task Force could not be located until the Sea

Aerial view of the search periscope and ESM mast of a UK *Resolution/Dreadnought* Class submarine. (US Navy)

The cruiser ARA *General Belgrano*. (*Armada Argentina*)

Harrier sortie described previously.

It is worth also mentioning that neither the intelligence information, nor the later positional information provided by the Sea Harrier, could help the British submarines make contact with the Argentine aircraft carrier on 2 May. Certain sources attribute this to communication problems. The submarines had to be close to the surface to be able to transmit and receive radio traffic either through a communications mast positioned on the sail or through a communications aerial trailed behind the submarine. As the reception and transmission of messages by means of the towed aerial was both difficult and slow, the submarine commanders sometimes preferred raising the communications mast.

Spartan had received the information regarding the position of TG 79.1, but although it had been located relatively close by, it was not possible to go and search for it as the carrier was in the zone of operations assigned to *Splendid*.

To avoid incidents of blue-on-blue, it is an old submariner's doctrine that two submarines do not occupy the same area of patrol at the same time. In the case of the Falklands/Malvinas, on 28 April (and taking the current locations of the submarines) the waters around the islands had been divided into sector squares and the three submarines present, HMS *Conqueror*, HMS *Spartan* and HMS *Splendid,* had each been assigned one of these areas. HMS *Splendid*'s CO, Commander Roger Lane-Nott explained:

> *Conqueror* was in the southern sector. *Splendid* and *Spartan* in the north, between Argentina and the Task Force...signals were exchanged with *Spartan* and they went to the east and we went to the west.

Conqueror was patrolling an area to the south, around 55° south and 65° west (close to Isla de los Estados). Meanwhile *Spartan* and *Splendid* were given a zone to the north of the Falkland Islands: The former was to patrol in the square located between 45° and 50° south, while the latter patrolled the remainder, but at the same latitude. The submarines were not permitted to go outside of their assigned area with the only exception being if they were following and in contact with an Argentine ship.

It is worth pointing out that the authority to make any modification to these rigid rules was not the responsibility of Admiral Woodward, but lay with the headquarters in the United Kingdom, 8,000 miles away from the zone of operations. The submarines formed part of Task Force 324, directly under the command of the Headquarters in Northwood, home of the Commander in Chief of the Fleet, at that moment occupied by Admiral John Fieldhouse, who delegated the direct control of the submarines involved in the operation to Vice Admiral Peter G. M. Herbert who occupied the post of Flag Officer Submarines.

Admiral Woodward wanted to interfere, surely realising that he was one of the most experienced submariners in the Royal Navy and was the appropriate person to adapt the current doctrine to the peculiarities of the naval war in the South Atlantic. And, he was there, down south. He tried to get the submarines released to search without boundaries to their areas of operations against surface targets. The only boundary that he tried to get put in place (to avoid any blue-on-blue incident) was that a British submarine would not be permitted to attack another submarine, at least not without unequivocally confirming first that it was not a nuclear one.

However, against the misgivings of the in-theatre commander of the TF 317, this was not authorised. This meant that the three submarines found themselves restricted to operating in squares that they had been ordered to patrol by Northwood.

Finally, HMS *Splendid* did not receive the intelligence information about the carrier's position until much later, when she found herself already out of position and unable to reach the Argentine Task Force.

The result of all of this was that none of the submarines were able to locate the Argentine carrier, let alone attack it. This would be a constant of the following days. Unfortunately for the Argentine Navy, however, much further to the south, the formation led by ARA *General Belgrano* would suffer the full force of the adversities of war.

Without knowing it, ARA *General Belgrano* had been located and tailed by HMS *Conqueror* for several days[3]. The pursuit had been made easy as the Argentine ships had not carried out even the most basic of anti-submarine manoeuvres. As expressed by the submarine's navigation officer, Jonathan "Jonty" Powis:

> We detected no sonar or radar transmissions...they did not go quickly, no more than 12 knots, they did not zigzag except for some very long leg gentle variations in course.

It is now known that, after a prolonged stake-out, which gave them the opportunity to visually confirm the identity of the Argentine ships, and having received the authorization from higher command to attack the *Belgrano* (really a 'second choice' since the aircraft carrier, the prime target, had still not been located), *Conqueror* launched three straight-run Mk 8 torpedoes, from 1,400 yards, at its prey. Two impacted the *General Belgrano*, while the third exploded close by the *Bouchard.*

Thus, with the sinking of the cruiser, the submarine threat, which the Argentine's own intelligence services had estimated to be up to three nuclear and one or two conventional (diesel-electric) submarines, had finally reared its head in the most brutal fashion.

The fact that the *25 de Mayo* had not met the same fate as the unfortunate *Belgrano* at the hands of another hunter of the deep was, to some extent, down to both circumstance and luck, as is usual in war. Professionalism and tenacity of the men responsible for providing anti-submarine protection for the *25 de Mayo,* and the decisions taken by its commander, had also helped increase its luck during those weeks.

When it came to the anti-submarine operations to protect the Argentine aircraft-carrier, one must bear in mind that these operations, whether or not they succeeded or failed, were not all about when an enemy submarine was detected and sunk, but more about managing to evade or impede a successful submarine attack while trying to defend against such an undersea force, as the events of those days bore out. After all, in anti-submarine warfare, the denial to the submarine of the possibility of attacking one's own units is equivalent, or more, than the sinking of the enemy.

The submarine is a weapon fundamentally used to deny the use of the sea. Its purpose is to sink the vessels that sail in the water under its control, or to threaten to do so in such a manner that nobody is prepared to take the risk. In the first days of May, they did not achieve their purpose, at least not regarding *25 de Mayo*. They were also unable to stop them returning to a secure base, with the possibility remaining that they could return to sea later, or that their Carrier Air Wing could be deployed to land bases and remain useful to the war effort.

At the operational level, the British submarine force bottled up the Argentine Navy and restricted its movement to shallow waters. However, at the tactical level and during the first ten days of May, the Argentine Navy had a minor victory and retained their operational capacity pretty much intact.

It should also be said that although the Argentine fleet took up a defensive posture from 2 May, its anti-submarine forces showed themselves to be more offensive than before.

2
BASICS OF ANTI-SUBMARINE WARFARE

From 17 February 1864, when in the US Civil War the Confederate submersible CSS *H. L. Hunley* sank the USS *Housatonic*, passing through both World Wars, the Cold War and dozens of regional conflicts right up to the present day, the submarine has caused an awful lot of anxiety amongst the sailors of all nations.

With its ability to deny its enemy the use of the oceans, the submarine played an important role in the First World War, then considerably increased its impact during the Second, especially in the blockades first of the British Isles (carried out by German *U-Boot*) and the Japanese mainland (by the United States "Silent Service"). During the Cold War, both nuclear-powered and conventional submarines of both sides carried out stealthy reconnaissance and espionage missions throughout the globe. In this way the submarine became, in less than a century, one of the primary weapons of any navy.

Having said this, it is not necessary to point out that the detection of a submerged enemy has become an art that has evolved ever since the day when the submarine first burst upon the naval scene.

During the infancy of anti-submarine warfare, it was necessary to rely on the ability of crew members to spot a mast breaking the surface and leaving a wake, or bubbles on the surface left by a diving submersible. This ability, as will be noticed later, continues to be useful to this day.

The end of the First World War brought with it the creation of the first versions of what we know today as sonar, even though at that time it really was not particularly effective given the enormous quantity of false contacts it gained, combined with its poor detection range.

The difficulty of submarine detection did not become so acute until the latter stages of the Second World War. By that stage, submersibles, in other words surface ships that could submerge when required to carry out or evade attack, were being developed into true submarines (vessels whose natural environment was the depths of oceans) with the introduction of the snorkel. This device permits a submarine to 'breathe' while submerged, and thereby to run its diesel engines while close to, but under, the surface of the water. These engines, the sole purpose of which were to recharge the submarine's batteries, required a constant supply of oxygen to operate. Until then, submersibles spent a large part of their patrol time on the surface, running the diesel engines to recharge its batteries and, therefore, could be located in the same way as a conventional warship.

Nuclear propulsion later provided another twist to the story, giving a submarine the ability to separate itself almost permanently from the surface of the sea.

These days a submarine spends its time almost permanently submerged and the time that it spends with some part of its superstructure exposed above the surface is minimal. Therefore, the most effective way to locate them is using sound waves.

Water either absorbs or reflects both electromagnetic energy from radar and light in a way that it is almost impossible to see a submarine under the surface, except in exceptional circumstances in shallow waters where the transparency of the water makes this possible.

However, sound can be used in multiple ways in water. In the first place, taking advantage of the fact that all submarines make some type of noise that can be picked out by expert human ears or, thanks to scientific developments, sophisticated equipment that can detect noise levels much more subtle than could be previously imagined.

The use of sound in this way is known as "passive sonar". It consists of a listening device which is characterised as having (in ideal conditions) a greater range of detection than active sonar, and is completely silent. However, it will only provide the direction of the contact from the device, and does not provide any information about its distance and course. However, this can be determined during a prolonged contact by means of analysis of the movement of the target (also known as "Target Motion Analysis" or TMA).

Modern sonar, differentiating it from its more primitive predecessors, is not only capable of listening to frequencies that are audible to the human ear, but can also monitor those inaudible frequencies that are both higher and lower. This equipment presents the results of a detection either on a printout or on a display so that they can be interpreted and analysed by the operator.

In addition to just trying to detect the presence of a non-natural object, passive sonar can also be used to attempt to classify the sound being emitted. To do this, it tries to decipher the acoustic signature which is unique and peculiar to each type of vessel, as they usually have distinctive types of engines and equipment which individually generate sound, both audible and not audible to the human ear.

The combinations of these sounds (which are generally of a low frequency) make up the acoustic signature, which can be deciphered, especially with the help of computer equipment. The classification of contacts by the sonar operator can be divided into the following categories:

1. Merchant ships
2. Warships
3. Smaller vessels
4. Submerged submarines
5. Biological sounds
6. Sounds and effects of the sea
7. Aircraft sounds

In the words of Héctor M. Carrizo, a Tracker acoustic operator:

> Each one of these emits a sound with a different tonal frequency and distinct distribution of harmonics that allow you, during an analysis, to classify the contact. Each vessel has its own acoustic signature, even ship of the same class. Everything depends on how close the sonar device is and what flank it is on. This makes it possible to identify each producer of a sound or signal. This information, along with a detailed collection of previous analyses, make some level of identification possible. This implies that to identify a submarine by its signature as, for example submarine X of class Y, you must have some previously gathered information about its signature. The leading navies in the art of anti-submarine warfare have spent a great deal of time collecting this kind of data about their possible opponents.

Different types have different characteristics, and this also permits the first approximate classification of a contact. Therefore, for example, it is common for a merchant ship to have two or three propellers with no more than four blades that rotate relatively slowly. Additionally, these propellers have various imperfections that make it easier to count the turns. The sound produced by the propellers is due to cavitation: this happens when the blades pass so quickly through the water that the water does not have time to completely cover the blade. In this case, the reduction of pressure on the outside part of the propeller blade produces bubbles which generate sound when they collapse.

On the other hand, a warship usually has two propellers with a good number of blades (as many as six), all of which have been balanced and produced free of imperfections. A submarine has between four and seven blades usually on a single propeller and in some cases, two. If it is submerged, its main characteristic is that it will present compressed cavitation: the rupture of the bubbles is faster and more violent. It should be added that the cavitation will be greater when the pressure of the water is less. In other words, the greater the depth the lesser the effect.

The characteristics of the propagation of sound are used by the sonar, but the behaviour of the sound in the water is not dictated by the sonar operator, but according to the logic of physics. With the sea being so heterogeneous with respect to factors that affect the propagation of sound, an operator will rarely have all the factors at his disposal with which to make a full classification. Temperature, depth, salinity, the presence of marine animals or flora in the water, and the proximity of other artefacts that produce noise has turned acoustic warfare into an art that requires a large amount of resource dedicated to it within a country's navy.

The other method of using sound in water involves the transmission of a pulse of controlled sound and the reception of an echo produced by the reflection of this pulse by an underwater object. This is known as 'active' sonar. The equipment measures the time that it takes the sound pulse to travel to, and return from, the target and, taking into account the speed at which sound moves in the water, it is therefore possible to work out the distance to the object. Using other mathematical calculations, it is also possible to work out the direction and so achieve an approximate location of a target.

If it seems that the active method has more advantages than the passive method, then one must consider that the 'ping' (the sound energy pulse produced by the equipment in the water and used to produce an echo) can itself be detected at a much larger distance than the sonar itself is able to detect the echo of a target it is searching for. In this way, not only does it give a submarine a warning that it is being hunted, but this 'ping' or pulse of sound can be used as a 'call light' and thus facilitate the detection of the transmitter itself.

Generally, sonar is associated with being connected to an operator in a surface vessel or submarine. The continual evolution of sonar technology has allowed what at first consisted of a fitting sticking out from the bottom of the hull of a warship to be developed into equipment that can be placed in a tube approximately one meter long and fifteen centimetres diameter. This device is called a sonobuoy.

The first sonobuoy was used by the US Navy in 1942, following its invention the previous year in the United Kingdom. Physically, a sonobuoy can be considered a combination of a simple sonar device with a buoy. It is launched into the sea by either a ship, helicopter or aircraft and, upon contact with the water, it deploys a radio aerial and releases, at a pre-set depth, an array of subaquatic microphones which are known as hydrophones. These buoys have evolved with the advent of the digital computer to the point that they have become established as the most efficient system for the detection of submarines.

In common with more traditional ship-borne sonar, sonobuoys can be both active and passive; and according to the relevant doctrine in use by their operators, active sonobuoys are generally used to precisely locate a contact that had previously been detected by passive methods.

In addition to the ubiquitous sonobuoy, there are also other methods for the detection of submarines that are not acoustic by nature.

In 1941, a device for detecting magnetic anomalies, the Magnetic Anomaly Detector (MAD) was introduced. This device detects modifications in the magnetic field of the Earth caused by the presence of a significant amount of a ferrous material, such as a submerged submarine. Although it possesses a very limited range of less than half nautical mile, making it a sensor that is not suitable for searching large areas of sea, it does become invaluable for determining the location of a submarine already detected by other methods. It permits an operator to come up with a location for an attack: when working out a solution for an attack on a submarine, it is necessary to know precisely where the submarine is due to the limited range of anti-submarine weapons.

The Second World War also saw the development of radar, some of which were optimised to search for periscopes. Another element in the possible methods of detecting a submarine, which should not be overlooked, is electronic warfare. This method works by detecting radar signals or conventional radio emissions emanating from submarines.

Finally, let's return to the first method we described. The eyes of observers, pilots and weapons operators have always been another important means of detection of submarines. On a clear day and with a calm sea, a submerged object can be detected if it is located close to the surface, of course depending on

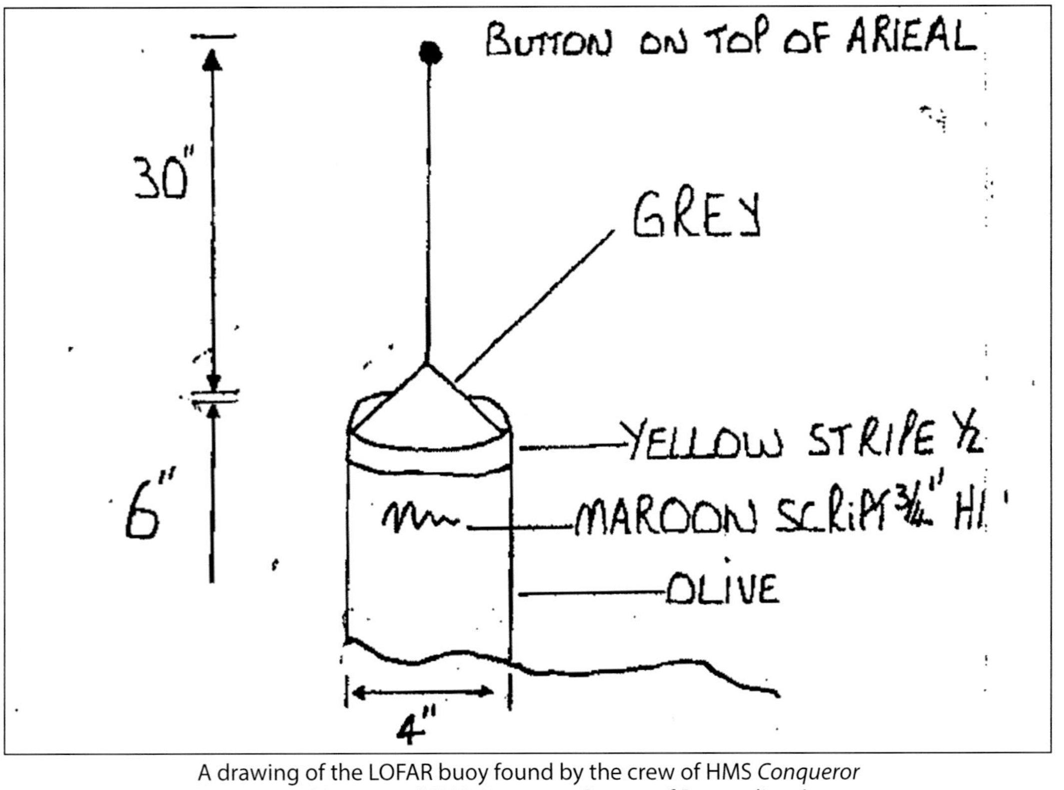

A drawing of the LOFAR buoy found by the crew of HMS *Conqueror* on 19 May 1982. (HMS *Conqueror* Report of Proceedings)

A dedicated anti-submarine aircraft, a US Navy S-2E Tracker of Anti-Submarine Squadron 33 (VS-33) – with its MAD boom extended and radar dome down – flying over submarine masts during an exercise in 1970. This same aircraft (BuNo 152829) was later sold to the Argentine Navy and given the code 2-AS-22. (US Navy)

the observer being almost perpendicular to the submarine to be able to overcome the natural refraction of light in the water.

It should always be born in mind that during observations of vast areas of oceans, it is possible to erroneously classify a whole host of objects and visual effects as submarines. For a crew member to be a 'qualified observer', he or she must spend numerous hours on searches, in addition to the corresponding academic preparation, before being deemed to be a reliable operator in anti-submarine operations. This subject cannot be taken lightly as it is commonplace for observations by non-qualified crew members to lead to long and fruitless search missions.

All of the above resources are available to the officer who has responsibility for carrying out operations in an anti-submarine war.

Now, the question must be addressed as to what happened with respect to the Argentine Navy in 1982.

3

ANTI-SUBMARINE ASSETS OF TASK FORCE 79.1

Sonar, radar and other anti-submarine equipment were found within the various units of the fleet and the Carrier Air Wing. However, most of the workload would fall on the four S-2E Tracker aircraft, and to a lesser extent on the two Sea Kings helicopters, both types being based on the aircraft carrier ARA *25 de Mayo*, as well as upon the destroyers ARA *Santísima Trinidad, Hércules* and *Py*.

It is worth adding that although the Task Force had some Aérospatiale Alouette III helicopters (also embarked on the aircraft carrier) and two Westland Lynx Mk 23 helicopters on the Type 42 destroyers (both from the First Helicopter Naval Air Squadron under the command of *Capitán de Corbeta* Augusto Rivolta), the main and important missions that these machines were tasked with were not anti-submarine duties. Having said this, Lynx 3-H-142, based on the destroyer ARA *Hércules*, in between its other assigned tasks, did carry out some visual and radar search sorties without detecting anything worthy of mention during the first days of May.

The Anti-Submarine Naval Air Squadron (*Escuadrilla Aeronaval Antisubmarina*)

During this tour of duty on board *25 de Mayo*, the squadron's assigned role was 'to carry out naval surface search and close anti-submarine support in order to provide protection for the surface units of the Task Force'.

The S-2E Tracker aircraft

The main role of the Grumman Tracker within the embarked Carrier Air Wing was anti-submarine search and attack.

The Tracker is a twin-engined high-wing aircraft, designed specifically to be operated from an aircraft carrier. It possessed a six-hour endurance at a maximum speed of 450 km/h (280 mph). In the cockpit, it had two side by side forward positions for the pilots (commander and co-pilot) and two further positions inside the fuselage for the sensor operators: one acoustic and one Radar/MAD/ESM (Electronic Support Measures). In the aircraft, the pilot has

A formation of recently received S-2E Tracker flying close to their home base. October 1978. (Via C. Mey)

the role of commander while the co-pilot is the operational control officer, in charge of navigation, crew coordination, communications and tactical computer management.

In 1978, six model 'E' aircraft were purchased from the US Navy as surplus to their requirements and were delivered by ferry flight direct from the USA, to replace the S-2A models that had been in use in the Argentine Navy since 1962.

The contract to purchase the aircraft included for the refurbishment and replacement, in full, of the aircraft systems over and above those considered to be life expired by their previous user. This was to be carried out by Grumman, the original manufacturer of the aircraft. The last US Navy unit using the Tracker, VS-37 squadron which operated S-2G aircraft, retired their aircraft in 1976. They had been replaced in service by the more modern Lockheed S-3 Viking.

Grumman made a huge effort to honour the contract signed with the Argentine Navy in its totality, the progress of which was closely monitored by Argentine officers. A good example of the lengths gone to by Grumman was a lack of technicians qualified in the overhaul of the antiquated AN/ASN-30 antisubmarine tracking computer, which had been constructed using electro-mechanical technology. To get them into working order once again, the factory had to rehire a technician who had previously worked on the computer and who was then living in South Korea. He was put to work with the old equipment and was finally able to get them to come back to life. As recalled by Gustavo Ottogalli, one of the officers that was supervising the work:

> The demands on the manufacturer were tremendous. Especially with the tactical computer, we wanted it to work exactly as the manual said, even if it was obsolete. The technician in charge was put under a lot of pressure, to such an extent that he started smoking again. In the end, everyone's effort paid off and the planes arrived in a condition as if they had been recently manufactured.

The aircraft entered service painted light grey on the upper surfaces and matt white on the lower, as per most aircraft in the Argentine Navy. Later during the conflict, the aircraft were repainted dark grey all over, with the aim of making them more difficult to be seen by enemy aircraft.

The most important improvement, over the previous version used by the Argentine Navy, was the AN/AQA-4A sonobuoy equipment. This had been developed as part of the project that was known in the United States as Project Jezebel. Compared to the "A" model of the Tracker, which used its radar as its main sensor, the newer version used acoustic detection and analysis to find and destroy submarines. The sonobuoy equipment the new aircraft possessed, although obsolete at the time of the introduction into the Argentine Navy (bearing in mind that the US Navy was by then already using the AN/AQA-7), gave the anti-submarine capability of the squadron a huge boost.

In older aircraft, if they were even equipped with sonobuoys, the operator had to literally listen directly to what was captured by them. The Jezebel system, otherwise known as LOFAR, which was the acronym of "Low Frequency Analysis and Recording", allowed the analysis of lower frequency sounds (inaudible to the human ear). These frequencies could be detected at greater distances due to their attributes of propagation in water. Through the analysis of the coherency of these frequencies over time, the Jezebel equipment permitted the detection of the presence of a submerged submarine, even though it was completely inaudible to the human ear. In other words, being able to listen to the spectrum the human ear cannot hear made the search for a submarine more precise and at greater distances.

The AQA-4A processor can make a simultaneous analysis of the sounds received from up to a maximum of four sonobuoys and displayed the results to an operator via lines made by a needle on photo-sensitive paper. This paper displays each frequency band from left to right. In this way, by running this readout over to a cylinder to roll it up, it was possible to visualise the behaviour of a determined frequency. This provided the possibility to 'listen' to a sound, frequency by frequency, and not as per the human ear that receives all the different frequencies that it is capable of hearing at the same time. Also, it could perform CODAR analysis (Correlation Detection and Recording): knowing the time at which the same sound arrives to two different sonobuoys, the system can provide a relatively precise location of the submerged contact.

The Jezebel/Tracker weapons system enabled the aircraft to monitor an area of 40 by 60 nautical miles, while a sonar system carried by a helicopter or located in the hull of a destroyer only permitted the detection of a submarine at range no greater than 5,000 yards. As indicated by one of the pilots of the Anti-Submarine Naval Air Squadron, the Jezebel system represented a new capacity for the squadron, equivalent to: 'what the Exocet represented for the attack pilots.'

However, the most surprising fact about the AQA-4A was that everything related to its introduction into service came from within the Argentine Navy, due to the US Navy not authorising the delivery

A Tracker being launched from ARA *25 de Mayo*. (via Enrique Fortini)

of the tactical use manuals.

Another milestone, described by the commander of the squadron as being a 'technical surprise', was the incorporation into the aircraft of a Tektronix 7L3 oscilloscope – a piece of equipment used for analysis of the frequency or intensity of signals.

These oscilloscopes were usually used for the calibration of radar, communication, and other electronic equipment. It was usually part of the outfit of a land-based laboratory. In other words, it was a piece of equipment that had been acquired by the Argentine Navy in small numbers for use in workshops and laboratories, but never with the intention of installing them into aircraft. However, needs meant that these were adapted to be fitted in aircraft to be used on combat operations. The original ESM equipment carried by the Tracker only had the ability to receive conventional radar signals (between 1,000 and 10,000 MHz), while the air search radars used by the Type 42 destroyers (which were used by both sides in the conflict and were the main sensor used by the fleets to detect aircraft) used "P" band. As the ESM equipment in the Tracker was deaf to this type radar, operation of this aircraft would be very dangerous as the crew would not know they were being illuminated by an enemy radar (that is to say, that it had been detected), which was an essential ability for a search aircraft.

The original intention was to use the AN/ALR-3 passive warning sensor fitted to the SP-2H Neptune aircraft, which can monitor the higher and lower frequencies, but it was both too heavy and too large to be fitted in the cabin of the Tracker. The fitting of this equipment would have meant that it would not have been possible to operate the Tracker from the aircraft carrier. It also did not afford much of a margin of security given its age.

The installation of the new ESM equipment was carried out on the initiative of the civilian engineers of the No. 2 Electronic Workshop in Base Aeronaval Comandante Espora (the main Argentine Naval Air Station). It was there that the aircraft were fitted with a small UHF aerial, which was connected directly to the Tektronix oscilloscope. Three oscilloscopes were available for fitting to aircraft, which had been retrieved from the workshops in Espora, Puerto Belgrano (the main Argentine Naval Base) and Buenos Aires.

These were mounted inside a hard case which had been modified so that it could be fitted into the aircraft without any problem. These 'new' oscilloscopes worked perfectly in their new habitat. The Tracker's operators quickly became proficient with their use, finally granted a margin of security necessary for combat operations. They also permitted the pilots to develop new flight profiles to fly under the detection lobe of the radar, as close as 18 miles from one of their own surface ships which, to the dismay of their crew, could not see the aircraft on their radar while from the Tracker they could perfectly observe the Type 42 destroyer that was being used for these trials.

It is worth pointing out that the equipment was fitted in the space that was used for the AQA-4A, which meant that the use of one meant the other was excluded.

At the same time, other modifications were made to the aircraft's own radar, an AN/APS-88, which operated in the "X" band. This radar had a maximum theoretical detection range of 240 nautical miles, and a range of 90 miles for a surface ship of the size of a destroyer. However, during the conflict, due to the problems in maintaining this equipment, this range never exceeded 70 miles. The doctrine for its use dictated that at certain points during the flight the aircraft would need to gain height and lower the radar dome (this was usually stowed inside the aircraft to obtain both a higher cruising speed and lower fuel consumption) and to emit no more than three revolutions of the antenna. With this, sufficient discretion was ensured to avoid interceptions or attacks by aircraft. Once the brief search was complete, the crew would immediately turn off the radar, raise the radome and descend rapidly. Then, once the ESM operator had informed the aircraft commander that the enemy unit had lost radar contact with the Tracker, they would immediately alter course, in one direction or another, by at least 45°, thereby avoiding a possible interception based

SSQ-47B sonobuoy and stowage case. (Peter Ellis)

on estimation of course.

The problem then arose, especially for an old analogue radar, that the operator had to remember, in the few moments that he received the information, all the useful data, such as location and distance of the echoes. To avoid mistakes and to reduce the workload of the crew member, a mount was constructed for a Polaroid instant camera so that a picture of the screen could be taken when the radar was emitting. These cameras were donated by an optician in Bahia Blanca, whose owner had been done his military service in the Argentine Navy. In this way the possible problems were minimised, especially when it came to the analysis of the information received.

It is also worth adding a comment about the aircraft's long-range navigation system. This was the VLF-Omega GNS 500 series 3, installed and tested in 1981, which enabled the aircraft to navigate with great precision up the limit of its operational radius. Even bearing in mind that all its navigation and attack equipment was analogue in the best of cases (and electro-mechanical in the worst), and in the same way that a relatively modern tactical computer had not yet been developed to better hunt submerged contacts, the "E" model of the Tracker provided the Argentine Navy with a capacity practically without equal in Latin America.

To recap the sensors used in anti-submarine warfare, the aircraft was fitted with an AN/APS-88A surface search radar; an AN/ALD-2B and a Tektronix 7L3 ESM, an AN/ASQ-10A MAD Sensor (with a range of 1,000 feet) in the aircraft tail; and finally, an AN/AQA-4 Acoustic Processing System. The connection between the aircraft and the sonobuoys was provided by an AN/ARR-52A receiver which had 31 channels.

The AQA-4A, was capable of monitoring 31 sonobuoys in total, four of them simultaneously.

The passive sonobuoys, or LOFAR, were either the US SSQ-41A, Canadian SSQ-527A or the French DSTV4 L/M. All of these models had a similar performance and there were considerable stocks of them both in the country and on-board of *25 de Mayo*.

They were both omni-directional and had a pre-configurable time of operation of one, three or eight hours. Once the selected time of operation had elapsed, they would stop transmitting and sink themselves. These sonobuoys also allowed the operator to pre-select the depth that the sonobuoys extended the hydrophones below the buoys. In use with the Tracker, the parameters of duration and depth of deployment of the sonobuoys needed to be set on the ground prior to take-off (on some other aircraft it is possible to make these setting in flight, thus giving a greater degree of flexibility in their use). It's worth observing that omni-directional sonobuoys detect frequencies without being able to determine the precise direction from which these are coming. In other words, there was no bearing to the contact.

A US Navy Douglas AD-4B Skyraider dropping a Mk. 44 torpedo during testing in March 1959. This type of torpedo was used by both sides during the 1982 war. (US Navy)

The active buoys were the US-made SSQ-47B or SSQ-552A (from Canada), which have a maximum lifespan of 30 minutes of operation in the water. However, during the operations carried out in May, only passive sonobuoys were used: when operating in shallow waters and using an active buoy, the picture on the receiver has a lot of clutter from the reflections of the sound wave from the ocean floor. Some years after the conflict, the Argentine Navy solved this problem by using digital sound processors (Project Minerva).

As the commander of the Tracker squadron recalled, 'the Tracker is a flying laboratory' which is trying to work out if there is a submerged submarine present by means of changes to the environment that are produced by its presence, as much by the noise it produces as by the

"MAD! MAD! MAD!" A S-2T Turbo Tracker detects a submarine with its Magnetic Anomaly Detector during an exercise in 2009. The S-2E fleet of the *Escuadrilla Aeronaval Antisubmarina* was refurbished by IAI with turboprop engines in the mid-nineties. (*Armada Argentina*)

Tracker 2-AS-23 aft of ARA *25 de Mayo*, being armed with a Mk. 54 depth charge. The picture was taken on 1 May 1982. (Via Juan José Membrana)

emissions it makes or by the changes in the magnetic field that it causes.

The Tracker's primary offensive capability was the Mk 44 Mod. 1 air-launched torpedo, two of which were carried in the weapons bay located in the belly of the aircraft. This US made torpedo, once released and in the water, automatically orientated itself in the direction of its target and was one of the most popular anti-submarine weapons in use in 1982, also being used by the Royal Navy.

These torpedoes would be launched from an aircraft at an altitude of between 300 and 900 feet and are stabilized in flight by a small parachute brake deployed from its tail and which is released upon contact with the water. This permits it to hit the sea at a relatively reduced velocity and a pre-determined angle which prevents damage to sensitive electronic components. The sonar seeker is protected by a plastic cover so that it is not damaged during the descent and which is ejected on impact with the water. Contact with the water activates an electric motor which can propel the torpedo at a speed of 30 knots, firstly in a descending helical search pattern, and then an ascending one whilst it emits with a small active sonar fitted in its nose. Whilst making its helical searches with a radius of approximately 1,300 feet, the sonar begins to transmit, seeking its prey. If it does not detect anything, it performs a flat reverse turn and continues with its search, always returning to the same direction of the initial turn. On detecting a target, it straightens out its course and begins to emit an almost constant sonar signal and directs itself towards the attack. At this point it arms itself and upon impact a 75-pound HBX warhead goes off against the hull of the submarine.

The range of the torpedo's sonar is 3,300 feet; therefore, its launch point must be very precise for the weapon to be effective, best if head-on or to the starboard side of a submarine and at not more than 2,500 feet. In doing so, as the torpedo turns towards the left, the probabilities of finding the target are greater.

The use of practice torpedoes, which have a data recorder in place of a warhead, was common before the Falklands/Malvinas War. However, the results achieved by these practice torpedoes were not very promising, despite the efforts of the weapons workshops. Faults were commonplace and on most occasions the torpedo was lost without trace, which made the analysis of the results of the test impossible. The crews did not have much confidence in the weapon, but they were more effective than dropping depth charges. A trial with

Tracker with folded wings, aboard the aircraft carrier. Behind it is an Alouette III helicopter. November 1981. (via Enrique Fortini)

a warhead fitted was never carried out due to a lack of suitable targets and a submarine test range.

As well as the torpedoes, while operating from the aircraft carrier and on anti-submarine missions, they could also carry anti-submarine depth charges and either Albatross or FFAR rockets under the wings.

The air-launched depth charges could be used to attack a submarine that was discovered on the surface or at periscope depth. It was necessary to be able to see the target otherwise depth charges would not be very effective. They could also serve as deterrent to a submarine, as the effect of the shock wave on the submarine hull could have a demoralising effect upon the crew.

During the conflict, the Argentine Navy used two different types of depth charges: the Mk 54 mod. 2 which was produced in the United States and BASA, or '*Bomba Antisubmarina Argentina*' (Argentine Antisubmarine bomb). These were both cylindrical bombs with a flat head, weighing 350 pounds (158 kg) and could be armed with either hydrostatic or contact fuses. The former type of fuse was used by the Argentine Trackers on anti-submarine missions. Their operating depth could only be set while on deck (but not in flight) between zero and 250 feet. These weapons had an effective radius, in other words the distance at which the effect on the submarine would be lethal, of about 115 feet.

To be effective, it was necessary to launch a pattern of at least four bombs with a separation between each bomb of 100 feet at an angle of 30° with respect to the submarine. In this way it was assured that with the imprecise aiming system fitted to the Tracker, at least one of the depth charges would land within its lethal radius. The aiming system of the Tracker consisted of a reticule painted onto the pilot's windscreen and a small aiming point fixed to the nose of the aircraft. With proper training, a pilot could release the depth charges using this system of aiming at an appropriate distance with a more likely degree of success.

Although a Tracker could carry up to four depth charges on its wings, during the conflict the squadron's aircraft operated with only two, both set for 50 feet (to impact on the hull of a submarine that was navigating at periscope depth).

The FFAR/Albatross (both 70mm rockets) were only effective against submarines on the surface. They were launched in a 15° dive, using the same aiming system as the depth charges and with an inert head with the sole purpose of piercing the submarine hull. However, it is unlikely that an inert 70mm rocket would perforate the steel hull of a submarine.

A Tracker being launched from *25 de Mayo* (by Carlos E. Cal)

The Grumman S-2E Tracker is a comfortable aircraft. The four air crew seats have quite a basic form, but with the ability to adjust them. However, they could be modified to be a bit more comfortable.

Besides this, the crew members were strapped in with shoulder straps and a belt which were all fitted into a four-way single release connector which also had a quick release lever to operate it easily. The seats also had a head support cushion; the main function, if not the only function, was to support the crew members' heads during the moment of being catapulted from the aircraft carrier.

The front seats also had a urinal function underneath them (a 'relief tube' according to the flight manual) which consisted of a black Bakelite cone connected to a tube leading to the exterior of the aircraft, which released the liquids by means of the difference in static pressure when the aircraft was in flight. The sonar operators who sat in the rear of the cabin had a similar device located to the right of the access door. The average flight time during the Falklands/Malvinas conflict was around 5 hours, so these devices provided a welcome relief for the crew. The concern of making risky flights in wartime, alongside the quantities of coffee that was habitually consumed by the crew, meant that these devices received regular use.

Returning to the operation of the Tracker, one of the most salient characteristics of the aircraft were the two Wright Cyclone R 1820-82C engines. Each of these engines produced 1,525 horsepower from their nine cylinders arranged in a radial fashion, were cooled by air and fitted with a three-bladed propeller.

As far as flight preparation went, this would start several hours before the planned take-off time. The maintenance crew, along with the armourers, would prepare the aircraft overnight so that there would not be any delays when it came to start up and take off. The aircraft would be moved up to the flight deck from the hangar, generally by

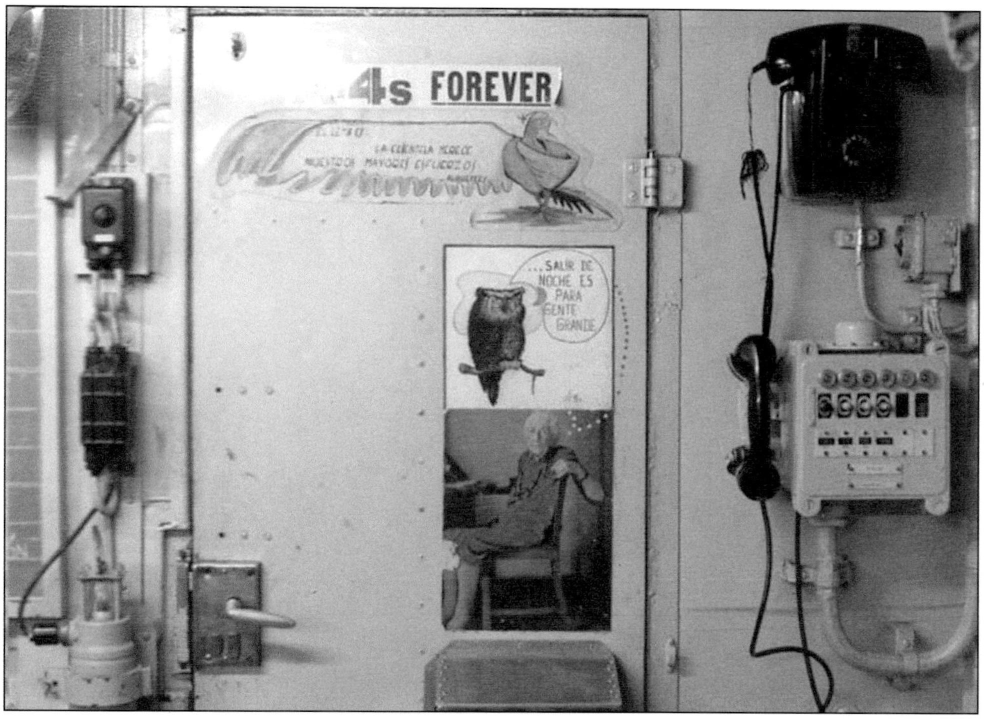

The door of the Pilot Ready Room on ARA *25 de Mayo*. The owl on the poster, the symbol of the *Escuadrilla Aeronaval Antisubmarina*, is saying 'going out at night is for grown-ups'. The members of the Skyhawk fighter-bomber Squadron glued a photo of an old woman below as a response. (via Enrique Fortini)

The Tracker 2-AS-25 is about to be launched on another sortie. Teniente de Navío M. Mariano Iriart, the deck officer in charge of the launch, is in the foreground. (Via Carlos Cal)

means of the lift in the bow of the ship, several hours before launch. This would enable the mechanics to carry out their pre-flight checks and test the engines and systems before the pilots and other crew members got into the aircraft. Usually all this preparation was carried out on the deck in darkness with no lights other than to dimly mark the limits of the flight deck. During the operations in the Falklands/Malvinas conflict, the submarine menace had reinforced discipline regarding light blackout, with the full knowledge of the consequences for the ship if it were to be detected due to this kind of indiscretion.

A back-up aircraft was also prepared in case of an unexpected technical fault in the primary aircraft, and was prepared so that if this were to happen, the crew would just have to get off one and on to the back-up with the least possible delay.

The pilots and operators would be summoned two hours before take-off to the Ready Pilots Room to receive instructions and last-minute data and then wait for the call from the Control Tower to board the planes.

The walk from the cabins in the stern to the pilot's briefing room, which was in the centre of the ship, was lit with red lights in order not to adversely affect the pilot's night vision.

The crew members would arrive dressed in their flight suits and generally were expecting to have a decent cup of coffee to wake up completely, although during these days a coffee was not so necessary to be completely alert, especially when about to go on a mission.

The pre-flight process would generally start with the weather information from one of the ship's forecasters, which was made especially difficult given the lack of data from the Pacific, due to this information being withheld by the Chileans and the United States. However, the meteorologists did their job well and the forecasts they provided were as complete and professional as possible given the circumstances.

The ship's Operations Department would then provide the necessary flight information; positions of friendly units and submarines; communication and authentication protocols; identification signals and recognition, all with the aim of providing sufficient information to be able to complete the mission in-hand. It would finish with a squadron pre-flight briefing with operational and logistics instructions, and the opportunity to refine the fuel-load calculations for each alternative aerodrome.

At the end of this process, the crew would finish by donning their anti-exposure survival suits, which were necessary to give a few extra minutes of life in the cold waters of the South Atlantic until the arrival of rescue units, in the case of ditching the aircraft in the sea. The suits were rather uncomfortable; besides having a fabric hood that expanded on contact with water in order to keep the wearer out of direct contact with the ocean, they also had tight rubber seals at the neck and wrists which were prone to causing edema in the hands and head. Underneath the flight suit the crew would usually wear a shirt, long johns and long woollen socks to protect themselves adequately from the cold. On top of the flight-suit, which was closed with a large waterproof zip, was a life vest which was in turn attached to the survival pack which contained such items as a first-aid kit, water, a knife, a .38" revolver, a flare pistol and individual smoke markers, all of which meant that the crew-members would feel a certain amount of protection.

The process of putting on all this equipment was like some kind of ceremony similar to the ritual performed when dressing a bullfighter

Tracker 2-AS-22 recovering onto the aircraft carrier. On the right, the Landing Signal Officer (LSO), perhaps *Capitán de Corbeta* Julio A. Covarrubias, is clearly visible. (*Armada Argentina*)

prior to going out to the bullring. A sense of invulnerability pervaded in the young spirits who used them, permitting a momentary pause in thinking about the real and present dangers that they were truly facing.

The leather flight jacket, with its typical patches, was worn over all this equipment to help to keep out the cold wind on the flight deck, until aboard the aircraft where it was hung up behind the seats.

The final piece of equipment that would be taken on-board the aircraft was the flight navigation briefcase. This would contain aeronautical and nautical charts, binoculars, some food and a Thermos containing coffee for the flight.

Forty-five minutes before the flight, when the aircraft was ready and flight deck prepared for operations, an imperative voice on the ship's intercom would announce: 'Tracker pilots to their aircraft!'.

At this moment, having signed the Aircraft Acceptance Form and verified the total aircraft weight and weapons load that it carried, the crew would leave to go to the aircraft, filling their flight bags with their helmets and other equipment.

The crew would inspect the exterior of the aircraft, illuminating it with torches that had a red filter over the lens. The low light provided would be sufficient to check the outside of the aircraft for the umpteenth time, always done with flight safety in mind. Once this routine had finished, they would climb into the aircraft via the small folding steps attached to the door on the side of the aircraft, below the right wing.

They would board in this order: pilot, co-pilot, operator 3 and then finally operator 4, each one would take their seat and begin the routine pre-flight checks once they were seated and buckled into their seats and their personal equipment plugged in.

The reading and completion of the pre-flight check-list before take-off and cabin preparation was the routine. From the Control Tower the speakers on the flight deck would announce: 'Tracker, start engines!'.

The pilot, having checked the area around the left-hand propeller, in coordination with the mechanic on the flight deck, rotated the blades with the starter, connected the magnetos and started to manually prime the engine until the explosions and the 1,525 HP Wright motor spat out burned oil from the lower cylinders into a puff of white smoke and the silence of the flight deck was now just a memory.

He would move the mixture lever to rich, disengage the primer and set the RPM to 1,200 for the initial warm up. The second motor would follow and after the disconnection of the 28-volt power hook up, they would put on their flight helmets and complete the cabin checks. Following this, the wings would be unfolded and a control check on the flying surfaces carried out: the flaps; landing hook; the weapons bay doors; and a final look into the engine nacelles by the mechanics to ensure that there were no leaks of either hydraulic fluid or fuel.

When this process was finished, the squadron mechanic, wearing a brown vest, would pass control of the aircraft over to the yellow vest wearing flight-deck controller. In times of peace it was usual to use this moment to carry out a check of the communications equipment, but during the conflict this could reveal the presence of the aircraft carrier. For this reason, everything was carried out in strict radio silence and with signals; if light permitted, by use of hand signals, and in darkness with a red torch. The handling of the aircraft was a synchronised ballet between the flight-deck personnel involved (including the youngest conscripts), and the pilots, all of which would take place without a single word being spoken.

With the aircraft still tied to the deck with chains, the engine checks would be finished. When completed, the flight-deck director would be informed and the chains removed. The aircraft would remain in place solely by the chocks on the wheels. If the ship's command had decided that the flight was to go ahead, the order would be given to remove the chocks and begin manoeuvring the aircraft to the catapult. On arrival, the Tracker would stop over the centre of the device. The catapult shuttle would run backwards under the front wheel, causing a slight sensation of a rising and falling of the nose from within the aircraft. At this point the holdback cable would be attached to the tail and the strobe, a specially prepared steel launching cable, would be connected between a hook on the belly of the aircraft and the catapult shuttle. The chocks that were holding the aircraft in position would then be removed and the pilot would release the brakes.

At this moment the catapult officer would take control of the operation and order the aircraft to apply full engine power. The throttles would be pushed forward until the engines were running at 3,200 RPM.

A check of the motor instruments would be made as well as a final check of the flying controls. Once ready, the co-pilot would give the catapult officer a salute. This officer, having checked all his control lights were green, would touch the flight deck with his hand, which was the order for the launch of the aircraft to be carried out. Then would come three wild seconds as the crew members' bodies were pushed back in their seats by the acceleration of the catapult and up they went. Airborne!

Training and experience on the Aircraft

All personnel of the Anti-Submarine Naval Air Squadron were obsessed with the destruction of subaquatic platforms, having a deep-seated belief of always pushing their training and material to the limit.

According to *Teniente de Navío* Enrique Fortini, Operations Officer of the squadron during the previous year:

> The squadron had possessed, from its creation, a refined professional mystique that had been increased gradually during 1979, 1980 and 1981 through the implementation of many projects to gain tangible improvements to the squadron personnel. We became proficient in the use of the AQA-4 Acoustic Processing System to such an extent that, with the use of Jezebel barriers, a new level of capacity in the anti-submarine warfare was attained. We felt we were the owners and exclusive users of an anti-submarine capacity that the rest of the aero-naval units in South America did not possess. We felt we were the new core of the Argentine Navy's anti-submarine warfare capacity. We were the top operators; we generated technical suggestions and tactics; we radiated professionalism and we were vehemently convinced that our ideas reached out beyond the horizon. Besides that, we were good.

The squadron certainly possessed a great level of knowledge of the aircraft they operated: they began operating the Tracker, beginning with the S-2A model in the 1960s. This prior knowledge of the aircraft helped the unit achieve in 1982, in the words of its commander *Capitán de Corbeta* Skare, '80 percent of its operational capability' in the new model. This had been achieved by various methods, the foremost of which was constant and demanding training.

Prior to the war, deployments to the aircraft carrier had been frequent and regular sorties carried out whilst embarked. It's worth noting that during 1981, almost all carrier landings were done at night. This was a matter of great pride for the squadron as this was, and still is, one of the most difficult and demanding manoeuvres in the aviation world.

As already mentioned, they regularly dropped practice torpedoes and at least once a year would carry out an exercise using homing torpedoes (without explosive heads fitted). Generally, these would be launched against a submerged Argentine submarine (which was at the same time practising torpedo evasion) but with the search head programmed so that the attack criteria were at a lesser depth than the submarine. This was to make it possible for the torpedo to detect the target but make it impossible to impact against it as its electronic programming would ensure that it remained above the same. This would not only prevent any kind of accident taking place, as well as making it possible (at least in theory) to recover the torpedo at the end of the exercise.

It is important to emphasise the continuity of training being carried out, which allowed the passing of knowledge from the senior crews to the less experienced, helping to augment the knowledge the latter brought from their training at the Naval Aviation Training School No 2 (*CAFA2*). It was also usual, for both pilots and operators, to be deployed aboard submarines of the Argentine Navy. This allowed them to put themselves in the shoes of their natural victim, in the process learning the virtues and limitations of the submarine as a weapon of war.

Another factor behind the high level of operational capacity came through the deployment during the territorial dispute with Chile in 1978.

During the crisis, the squadron was embarked on the aircraft carrier with its new S-2Es and carried out intensive anti-submarine operations with the backdrop of a situation that was a few hours away from becoming a full-blown conflict. This allowed it to fine-tune

ARA *Independencia* (ex-HMS *Warrior*), operating with S-2A Trackers from *Escuadrilla Aeronaval Antisubmarina. Independencia* was the Argentine Navy's first aircraft carrier and was in service between 1958 and 1969. (*Armada Argentina*)

A Lockheed P-3C Orion from Patrol Squadron 56 (VP-56) at Keflavik, Iceland, in 1977. (US Navy)

certain procedures and gain valuable experience, especially in the handling of the recently incorporated acoustic equipment that would later be used in the Falklands/Malvinas.

The main anti-submarine action during the crisis occurred in the first hour of 16 December when one of the Trackers tried to attack a submerged target with torpedoes. Although the attack run was carried out according to doctrine, the torpedo did not activate upon contact with the water, due to an error made during the loading of the weapon in the bomb bay of the aircraft. It's possible that this same submarine was also attacked by a Sea King helicopter and finally chased by a destroyer, which managed to hit it with one of its hedgehog rounds.

It was also possibly detected later in the afternoon by two Tracker aircraft, which attempted to attack it without finally being able to do so. This was recalled by Héctor Carrizo, who at the time was an NCO acoustic operator aboard the aircraft 2-AS-23, piloted by *Teniente de Navío* Covarrubias, which spent four hours orbiting the contact:

> We were launched around four that day to deploy a curtain of sonobuoys to the northwest, close to Isla de los Estados. The material objective of this sortie was a snorkelling submarine that had been attacked in the morning by destroyer ARA *Rosales*, which was part of the ASW screen for the aircraft carrier. According to the crew of the destroyer, at least one of its hedgehog mortars had impacted on the submarine and it might possibly have been damaged.
>
> While the commander and the co-pilot, *Teniente de Fragata* Daniel Bulló, covered the area with eight-hour sonobuoys, I monitored them as they hit the water to check if they were working or not. To my great surprise on monitoring, I believe, the fourth sonobuoy, I picked up a light cavitation that appeared to be coming from a submarine; and immediately reported it and within seconds all four of us were listening to it.
>
> The commander ordered us to prepare to initiate CODAR tactics and dropped a cross pattern of sonobuoys with 350 feet separation. From that moment some things began to fail; only one of the pairs of sonobuoys was working but gave us a strong and definite signal. We continued with other attempts while the signal was weakening and at this moment the squadron commander in 2-AS-25 arrived and took over as Scene of Action Commander and decided to change tactics from passive to active and follow the procedure carried over from the S-2As and began to transmit with the radar. A few seconds later we lost the only signal and stopped hearing the cavitation. We did not manage to re-establish contact.

The little knowledge the *Escuadrilla Aeronaval Antisubmarina* had regarding a nuclear submarine was thanks to USS *Thomas Jefferson* (SSBN-618) which took part in the 1981 UNITAS naval exercise. Here it is seen underway on 14 June 1976. (US Navy)

> On return to the carrier, we investigated what might have happened to our sonobuoys. We realised that we were dropping them too far apart and mixing up different models. It was an important lesson.

The squadron also carried out various reconnaissance missions:

> The crisis of 1978 got worse and reconnaissance flights took place night after night, culminating one dawn in December when my friend and co-pilot Marcelo "Chelo" Alvarez caught and surprised submarine ARCH *Simpson* on the surface with our search light while they were carrying out repairs between Isla Picton and Puerto

Toro. (Enrique Fortini)

Another excellent opportunity to learn was during the month-long visit, in 1981, of antisubmarine aircraft of the US Navy. The US Navy deployed two P-3C Orion of the experienced VP-56 "Dragons" squadron, then based in Jacksonville, Florida. Their presence was taken advantage of by eager members of the squadron: as the squadron commander would later remember in relation to the visitors from the north, 'certainly, they had a lot of answers and we had a lot of questions to ask'.

Without doubt, the experience led to an improvement in the tactics employed. In summary, the quantity of hours flown and the hunting spirit that characterised the squadron provided a great boost to morale in their conventional anti-submarine role as remember by Gustavo Ottogalli, one of the pilots: 'The training was so good that during combat missions we always had the answer to the tactical problem before us.'

Of course, the training or doctrine for dealing with a nuclear-powered submarine did not yet exist and had to be improvised.

The squadron during Operation *Rosario*

The squadron received its first warning of the forthcoming Falklands/Malvinas assault a few days before the start of Operation *Rosario* (the name of the Argentine operation to seize the islands), which left it little time to adjust procedures and work on the material.

Four Trackers were embarked on the aircraft carrier and carried out a total of seven surface reconnaissance missions between them (a total of 30 hours flying time), that served to supplement the information gained by the twin-engine Neptunes which carried out the main part of the long-range recce for the fleet.

Once the islands had been taken, an aircraft section (2-AS-22 and 2-AS-25) under the command of the squadron XO, *Capitán de Corbeta* Julio A. Covarrubias, operated from the airport at the island's capital, carrying out reconnaissance tasks. This detachment was organised off the cuff, and the squadron's personnel arrived there only with what they carried with them, as one of the crew members recalled:

> The order arrived to send a detachment to the recently occupied Port Stanley (or Puerto Argentino), and we landed there without any equipment. Luckily, I bumped into a Marine friend of mine who was in the process of returning to the mainland, and he left me his sleeping bag and overcoat – I only had my flight jacket and I was really suffering badly from cold. (Gustavo Ottogalli).

After performing eight operational sorties, both Trackers returned to Espora on 13 April. The aircraft that had remained on the aircraft carrier had already returned there on the 5th.

While in their home base, between 13 and 18 April six additional pilots were incorporated into the squadron as reinforcements (all of whom were previous members of the squadron who had gone on to other units), while at the same time installing the new ESM equipment. The aircraft carrier left port once again on 18 April and this short trip (the ship returned to port on the 25th) was used to requalify the returning pilots and brush up on operational tactics.

On 28 April the carrier once again sailed from port at 0920 hrs, and the squadron embarked once again, landing the available units on board around 1200 hrs, following a short flight from Espora.

Status of the aircraft in May 1982

Given the general condition of the Trackers in 1982, by May they were experiencing continual problems with their complicated engines. Such problems generally left only two serviceable aircraft available at any moment.

The squadron, as with other Argentine military units, had suffered because of the US embargo of arms and war material (in place since 1977 and which had begun to be relaxed in 1981 – but didn't stop the new Trackers arriving) even though in this case there were certain provisions which helped get around the consequences of the embargo.

With the skill and ingenuity of the technicians it was possible to overcome new complications that arose in certain problematic parts such as the CSD (Constant Speed Drive), which is a sealed unit that converted power from a variable speed engine into a constant speed to drive the alternators, so they could provide a constant 115v at a fixed frequency of 400 cycles to power the electronic equipment. Such equipment, given its complexity, was usually sent to be repaired in the United States. In the case of the CSD, through trial and error (neither manual nor test equipment was available), it became possible to repair them in Argentina which enabled aircraft not to be taken out of service due to their repeated failures.

In summary, even though the aircraft were being flown a lot, with a low number of hours remaining until their next inspection and with the embargo in place, the four aircraft that were embarked on the detachment that began on 28 April were 2-AS-22, 2-AS-23 (which had some technical limitations as will be described later), 2-AS-24 and 2-AS-26.

It's worth adding that 2-AS-21 did not fly during the conflict and 2-AS-25 was not available following its participation in the capture of the islands, and was only reincorporated into the squadron on 13 May.

The Second Helicopter Naval Air Squadron (*Segunda Escuadrilla Aeronaval de Helicópteros*)

The Second Helicopter Naval Air Squadron had the mission to 'carry out airborne anti-submarine operations and helicopter transport missions during the recapture and defence of the Falkland Islands'.

The Sea King Helicopter

The S-61D-4 Sea King helicopters (usually known as H-3 within the Argentine Navy) had been acquired new by the Navy in 1972, to be used for anti-submarine work from the aircraft carrier[1].

It is a twin-engine large helicopter that had first entered service in 1962 and that during the 1980s was the primary anti-submarine helicopter in both the US and Royal Navy. It had a maximum speed of 267 km/h (166 Mph) and a range of approximately 540 nautical miles. It had side by side positions for the pilot and co-pilot, and two positions aft for the anti-submarine sensor operators.

The main ASW equipment was the Bendix AN/AQS-13A (active/passive) dipping sonar, operating on a frequency of 13 kilocycles. This was lowered from the helicopter when in a stationary hover over the surface of the sea (at a height of approximately 30 feet) and placed the transducer (the part of the equipment that contained the hydrophones) under the surface, and from there listened to possible surface or submerged contacts. It had a range of approximately 5,000 yards and could be lowered to a depth of 500 feet.

At the same time, its ability to attack targets was provided with Mk 44 torpedoes or depth charges, which were carried on externally mounted pylons.

The H-3s were also painted in the same colour scheme as used by the Trackers, light grey on the upper surfaces and matt white on the undersides. One of them was painted, at some point in May in time for the *Operación Borbón* (the rescue of personnel from the airfield on Pebble Island/Isla Borbón), in a greyish blue, which is the colour they are still painted at the time of writing.

Sea King 2-H-234 operating from the Argentine aircraft carrier. (*Armada Argentina*)

Status of the aircraft in May 1982

Although the Sea King was a modern helicopter, the embargo on war material by the United States had brought some problems with the supply of spare parts, which greatly limited the training on it.

1981 had been a bad year for the squadron as they were left with just one of the five helicopters in their inventory in an operational condition. The rest had been cannibalised to maintain this single machine on the flight line.

Especially problematic (defined by one if its pilots as being 'untrustworthy') was the automatic cable hover system, which prevented nocturnal anti-submarine missions from taking place. This type of mission is one of the most difficult tasks that can be assigned to a helicopter as it requires the helicopter to maintain a stationary hover at a height of 30 feet from the surface of the sea during a search. This is very difficult to achieve in a night flight, bearing in mind in such conditions the pilot lacks any kind of visual reference and it is very easy to confuse the sea with the sky, as the horizon is not clear in these conditions.

The lack of trust in the automatic cable hover system, which, as characterised by its name, automates the process by which the helicopter maintains a pre-determined altitude whilst in stationary flight, hugely limited the night-time capability of the squadron.

Considering the scarcity of serviceable aircraft, and the problems with the stationary hover systems, it is therefore not surprising that the crews were not currently qualified for nocturnal anti-submarine operations, which caused great complications given that there were few hours of daylight at that time of the year. However, thanks to a great effort, four aircraft commanders qualified for this task by the middle of May.

There was also another problem. By mid-1982, a group of helicopter crews was scheduled to be sent to the UK to train on the Lynx helicopters that were due to be introduced a short time after. These were planned to be based on the Meko 360 destroyers, then under construction in Germany. To prepare for this posting, a certain number of experienced pilots had been transferred to the First Helicopter Naval Air Squadron, which limited the number of personnel available to operate the Sea Kings.

The final point to consider with regards to the Sea Kings of Second Helicopter Naval Air Squadron is that although the aircraft were acquired principally to improve the anti-submarine capacity of the fleet, their use in their secondary role (as happens in most navies which lack abundant resources) ended up absorbing the time of the machines, crews, and mechanics. As *Teniente de Navío* Guillermo Iglesias recalled:

> The squadron was, before the war, dedicated to tasks away [from] ASW, which on many occasions required the removal of the anti-submarine equipment, such as the AQS-13A sonar system which, of course, led to inevitable calibration problems and equipment failures.

An example of such non-anti-submarine missions, which interfered with their primary role, was over-land SAR (Search and Rescue). Whenever there was a natural disaster on the mainland, the H-3s would usually be present, often with their sonar equipment removed to increase their endurance and lift capability and at other times, even worse, with the sonar still fitted. It wasn't at all strange to find one of the helicopters rescuing a pregnant woman, about to give birth, being lifted from a train stranded by snow somewhere in the Andes, or helping to search for a group of lost mountaineers, or participating in rescue missions during flooding in another part of the country.

Then there was the requirement to provide support to the Argentine Antarctic bases during the Antarctic summer, especially from 1979, which also interfered with the anti-submarine readiness. This requirement took up between 60 and 100 percent of their resources for a period of three to four months of the year.

Sea King 2-H-231 dipping its AQS-13A sonar transducer during a training sortie. It was bought brand new in 1972 and flew until 1986. It is now preserved in the Argentine *Museo de la Aviación Naval*. (*Armada Argentina*)

Other work included the transportation of personal and the support of training missions for the Argentine Marines and Army.

In other words, besides the problems with the supply of spares, it was true that the main task of this anti-submarine unit had been becoming less important over the years.

The Squadron during Operation *Rosario*.

The squadron was taken by surprise when they found out about the forthcoming Operation *Rosario*. As already mentioned, at this moment there was a lack of proficiency, especially in anti-submarine warfare, given the lack of assets.

By means of a maximum effort by the technicians (and, in some cases, an administrative extension of life of some key components), and the return of some of the pilots from other postings, the squadron managed to prepare two aircraft to take part in this operation: 2-H-231 based on the ice-breaker ARA *Almirante Irizar* (in a troop transport role) and 2-H-234, based on board ARA *25 de Mayo*. Both machines were configured for transportation duties, without any sonar equipment fitted.

Sea King 2-H-231 had an important role during the taking of the islands. After a perilous journey to the islands on board the ice-breaker (the straps holding an Argentine Army Puma helicopter, that was located alongside it in the ship's hangar, broke and it partially damaged the fuselage of the H-3 – fortunately, the latter suffered only light damage, but the Puma had to undergo a major repair) 2-H-231 was the first Argentine aircraft to land on the islands soon after the conflict had started.

On 2 April, the helicopter carried out 18 sorties (a total of eight hours and ten minutes flying time), landing 197 men, eight drums of fuel and the evacuation of one wounded soldier. Later, it also took part in the occupation of other settlements in the islands, transporting both army personnel and marines.

Having completed its role in the taking of the islands, both helicopters arrived back at *Base Aeronaval Comandante Espora* on 7 April. The squadron remained there between 8 and 16 April, completing their training and carrying out eight flights to check out equipment and systems. Also, around this time, an important number of spares were purchased (from some civilian suppliers based in the US) which enabled the condition of the aircraft to be improved. It's also worth mentioning that, during this period, the H-3s were returned to their anti-submarine configuration with the reinstallation and calibration of the sonar equipment.

On 17 April, the two airworthy helicopters (once again, 2-H-231 and 2-H-234) were embarked on the aircraft carrier around midday, with the remaining crews and mechanics arriving that night. The time spend on board was optimised to continue with training, with two sorties being flown by two helicopters on the 20th, each one for technical training in anti-submarine tactics: the systems were functioning correctly and a contact at 16,000 yards was achieved on a corvette that was sailing at a speed of 12 knots.

The main tactical problem the squadron had was how to best develop a valid doctrine to be able to make the most of the Sea King's passive sonar capability. Pre-war training had focused purely on the use of the sonar in an active mode, but it became know that the commander of the Task Force, facing the threat of nuclear hunter-killer submarines (which were able to move at great speed) would limit the use of the sonar equipment to passive mode only. This is effectively what took place.

The squadron began to improvise doctrine for using the sonar in the passive mode. The tactic that resulted involved pairs of helicopters working together. While the first helicopter listened, the second one would go further forward in the direction of the possible contact the first one had established and would dip its sonar, with the intention of gaining contact with the possible submerged submarine. In other words, the submarine would be located somewhere between the two helicopters. Then they would attempt to close the distance until they were able to fix a position and carry out an attack.

The training continued during the following days, until the aircraft

AN/AQS-13 sonar control panel inside an US Navy SH-3H Sea King in 1987. (US Navy)

ARA *Santísima Trinidad* alongside HMS *Newcastle*, both Type 42 Destroyers, in Portsmouth, September 1981. The Argentine ship was tuning its 909 radars and its Sea Dart missiles. On 12 and 13 October it would make two successful missile launches. (*Armada Argentina*)

carrier arrived back at port on 25 April, and the helicopters returned to base the next day. On the 28th, they were given the order to embark once again, and the same two helicopters arrived aboard at 1008 hrs.

Two days later, with the aircraft carrier already getting close to the British fleet, the squadron readied the aircraft: one at 30 minutes alert and the other at five minutes, to be able to carry out anti-submarine/anti-surface and rescue duties, organising four crews to cover these operations. At the same time the mechanics and sonar operators began to work shifts of eight hours on, eight hours off.

Although there were issues with both training and supplies, a maximum effort was made to optimise existing resources to be able to carry out in the best way possible any future operations that would come their way. One of the pilots would comment that the level of training reached during this time was 'adequate' and that they were now ready to face whichever contingencies of modern naval warfare that would come their way. However, the one thing that wasn't lacking within the squadron was confidence.

Destroyers ARA *Santísima Trinidad* and ARA *Hércules*

ARA *Hércules*, coded D1, had been incorporated into the Argentine Navy in 1976 with its twin, ARA *Santísima Trinidad* (D2), joining in July 1981. They were the most modern vessels in the Argentine surface fleet.

The latter of the two had been constructed in the shipyard in Rio Santiago (Argentina), its construction having been delayed by an attack carried out by the Montoneros terrorist band. *Hércules*, on the other hand, had been constructed in the Vickers shipyard in Barrow-in-Furness in the UK – the same shipyard where the submarines HMS *Spartan* and HMS *Splendid* had been built. Curiously, Cammel Laird's shipyard in Birkenhead was the place that two other protagonists in this story were constructed: the aircraft-carrier *25 de Mayo* and the submarine HMS *Conqueror*. The antagonists in 1982 found themselves, one way or another, to be brothers in birthplace.

The design of the destroyers was the same as the Type 42 destroyers of the Royal Navy (as HMS *Sheffield* and HMS *Coventry* that would later be lost in the conflict) and were designed to be multi-purpose destroyers with an emphasis on air defence, for which they were equipped with the Sea Dart missile system. The Argentine Navy also had asked for MM-38 Exocet missiles to be installed on the ships (something lacking on their British counterparts), which would give them an increased anti-surface capacity, although it's worth adding that these had only been fitted to *Hércules*.

The two destroyers were still in the process of being accepted and incorporated into the fleet, and their full capacities were still unknown. Part of the crew that were on these ships had been on training courses in the United Kingdom until only a few weeks before the conflict.

In the way of anti-submarine sensors, the two ships were fitted with the Graseby Type 184M active/passive search and attack sonars and, in addition, the Kelvin Hughes Type 162M sonars for contact classification. In its passive mode, it was calculated that the 184M sonar had a practicable range not exceeding 1,500 yards, and some 3,500 to 4,000 yards in active mode.

They were also equipped with Marconi 992Q and Kelvin Hughes 1006 surface search and navigation radars and a Racal RDL 257 equipment for electronic countermeasures (ECM) and electronic support measures (ESM), which permitted them to be able to intercept and analyse signals received in the 1 to 18 GHz range.

Their armament to attack submerged targets consisted of two Mk 32 triple 324mm torpedo launchers which were fitted with Whitehead A244/S homing torpedoes, a generation later than the Mk 44s already described, and then the most modern torpedoes in the Argentine Navy's inventory (and possibly in the whole of South America).

Destroyer ARA *Hércules* entering *Base Naval Puerto Belgrano,* the largest base of the Argentine Navy. (*Armada Argentina*)

Destroyer D-27 ARA *Py* at speed. The Mk. 10 Hedgehog ASW mortar and the two Mk. 32 Mod 5 triple torpedo tubes are clearly visible in this photograph. ARA *Py* was struck off the Argentine Navy inventory on 31 January 1984 and sunk as a target on 15 June 1987. (*Armada Argentina*)

In summary, the two destroyers were well equipped and modern platforms, limited only by the limited knowledge in the operation of them by their crews.

During Operation *Rosario* the destroyers had formed part of Task Force 40.3, which had escorted the amphibious units directly involved in the taking of the islands.

Destroyer ARA *Py*

Destroyer D27 ARA *Py* had been incorporated into the Argentine Navy in 1973. It was formerly a United States Navy Gearing Class destroyer. It was built in 1944 and had participated in the last months of the Second World War and later the Korean and Vietnamese wars, bearing the name USS *Perkins*.

When it entered Argentine Navy service, although it had already been modernised to the FRAM II standard (which was carried out in the United States to improve the capacity of the old destroyers, in the context that the US Navy expected to have to deal with a massive number of Soviet submarines), it's equipment and sensors were already considered to be obsolete.

The ship, known some time ago as the 'Great Submarine Hunter' was in the final stage of her life. *Py* was finally retired from service in 1984 and in 1987 met its end as a target ship for a torpedo attack by the submarine ARA *Santa Cruz*.

It was fitted with an effective, but old, AN/SQS-23 sonar, designed and built at the end of the 1950s and known as the '10,000 yards sonar' thanks to its then innovative design. Obviously, its capacity had diminished to both its age and the US embargo, although it was still considered the best hull-mounted sonar in the Argentine Navy.

For conducting surface searches, it was equipped with an AN/SPS-10 radar, complemented by a AN/WLR1-3 ESM outfit. And, for anti-submarine purposes, it was fitted with two triple torpedo launchers (for Mk 44 torpedoes), depth charge launchers in the stern and a Mk 10 Hedgehog system.

During Operation *Rosario*, the *Py* escorted ARA *25 de Mayo*.

Argentine ASW-Tactics

In the 19th century the Royal Navy had been the world model to follow and many of the Argentine Navy's first commanders were moulded in the British school. Following the Second World War, the focus of attention had shifted to the US Navy and a large part of its doctrine and procedures had been adopted by the Argentine Navy.

However, there was a huge difference between the requirements and capabilities of the Argentine Navy compared to the Royal Navy or the US Navy, especially regarding carrier operations.

At the beginning of the 1980s, a US Carrier Battle Group would be centred on a large aircraft carrier which would usually carry between 60 and 80 aircraft. It would also have an anti-submarine protection screen that would consist of between 5 and 8 frigates and destroyers which would be deployed in a tactical formation to provide a deep layer of defence. The escort vessels, which according to the situation

Aircraft carrier USS *Dwight D. Eisenhower* (CVN-69) and its escorts in 1982. It had been offered to the UK on 3 May 1982, 'an offer that we found more encouraging than practical' according to Prime Minister Margaret Thatcher. (US DoD)

and circumstances carried out tactics of active or passive sonar, were aided by the aircraft and helicopters of the Carrier Air Wing, as well as by their own helicopters.

The anti-submarine aircraft of a USN Carrier Air Wing (at the time of the war it was the Lockheed S-3 Viking) would launch and monitor sonobuoys deployed on the edges of the formation, at a great distance from the centre of the Battle Group. At the same time the embarked helicopters, either Sea Kings or Kaman Seasprites, would busy themselves with the anti-submarine protection near the main body using their dipping sonars. In a combat situation, no fewer than ten aircraft would be in the air at any one time searching for submerged threats.

On the outer ring of this formation, at almost 100 nautical miles from the main body and covering its line of advance, one or two nuclear-powered attack submarines would also be operating as pickets.

In addition to all of this, there would be support from land-based aircraft, satellite reconnaissance and other measures, all using the latest and best available technologies.

As noted, the assets available to the Argentine Task Force were much humbler: just three destroyers, two anti-submarine helicopters and a few piston-engine aircraft supplemented by a few Argentine Air Force aircraft.

Furthermore, although there were few anti-submarine platforms, they also had to carry out tasks that were far from their speciality, such as surface reconnaissance and transportation of cargo. When it came to it, the US Navy doctrine that had been adopted had to be adapted to the requirements of the Argentine Navy in the problematic South Atlantic waters.

To make matters even worse, in May 1982, they were up against nuclear-powered submarines, a foe that had never been considered in the doctrine in use. The maximum speed of a nuclear-powered submarine (in general terms more than 30 knots) was vastly superior to what could be achieved by the Argentine Task Force, given the poor state of the aircraft carrier's propulsion system limited its sustained speed to 18 knots.

A Skyhawk recovering onto ARA *25 de Mayo*, while S-2E Tracker 2-AS-25 is parked with its wings folded. Early April 1982. (Via Juan José Membrana)

This speed difference would allow the submarine to attack almost with impunity, considering that the escort shield, having few ships, was unable to provide a 360° protection ring around the main body. Therefore, the aircraft carrier would always be vulnerable on one of its flanks or to its rear.

This, of course, hadn't been a problem for the Argentine Navy in their pre-war exercises, with the only submerged threat coming in the shape of conventional submarines, which of course when submerged (and being powered by batteries) were not capable of matching the speed of the surface group.

When dealing with conventional submarines the LAA (Limiting Approach Angle) of a submarine, which is a calculation based on the speed of the submarine to get within a given range of a target moving at a given speed, is taken into account. This angle, along with the range of the submarine's torpedoes, fixes an area in which to position the escorts and other protection units, whether they are surface vessels or aircraft.

However, when dealing with a nuclear-powered submarine the LAA does not apply, as the fact is that the speed of the submarine would be greater than that of the target and there is no time limit on submarine's endurance. In other words, if the threat comes in the form of a nuclear-powered submarine, the concept of the LAA disappears and the flank and rear of the force would be completely unprotected. *Contraalmirante* Allara was aware of this, as he described in his post-war report:

> The maximum speed of my Task Force was no greater than 20 knots and in the case of the older destroyers there were serious doubts as to their ability to maintain a sustained high speed due to the poor condition of their power plants. The 30 knots speed the enemy's nuclear-powered submarines could have handed them a factor of force that was impossible to neutralise both in terms of their ability to attack as for their ability to reposition.

At the same time, the equipment was neither adequate nor calibrated to counter a nuclear-powered submarine.

The only experience that the Argentine Navy had came from short exchanges with the US Navy, or by taking advantage of the presence of US submarines during joint exercises when carrying out an unauthorised MAD search or briefly registering an acoustic signature.

As noted before, thanks to its high speed, a nuclear-powered submarine can change its position quite easily, which also makes it tactically different from a conventional one, which needs to wait in a focal point for the enemy forces. This needs to be borne in mind when searching for the new threat which, although it might have already had its location detected, within a few hours it is able to move a great distance away from this location.

The high command of the Argentine Navy was very aware of this, and so from 2 May the anti-submarine protection of the fleet took different measures that complimented the generic measures that had been previously adopted.

Therefore, the formation adopted would be led at the front by destroyer ARA *Py* (there was a lot of confidence in its sonar capability), with the two Type 42 destroyers deployed on either flank. In the middle of the formation, at a distance of between 2 and 5 miles from its escorts, the high-value unit (the *25 de Mayo*) would be located.

For its protection, TG 79.1 used one of the oldest anti-submarine techniques, which was none other than to sail at the greatest speed possible and use a zig-zag manoeuvre. They were also instructed to travel in shallow waters (no more than 400 feet in depth at most – and at the shallowest depth possible) which would be dangerous for all types of submarines, but especially so for nuclear-powered ones given their higher speeds. This meant that parts of its progress were within sight of the coast and in some cases the ships' propellers stirred up the mud underneath them, so shallow were they sailing. *Contraalmirante* Allara wrote:

> As we did not have much information on the characteristics and capabilities of the enemy's nuclear submarines, my Staff came up with a chart of limitations to be used in the area of operations. The chart was used to make sure the movements of our own forces were done in a way that was favourable for anti-submarine protection. For example, at depths below 120 metres a nuclear submarine safe operating speed would be limited to 15 knots and their maximum safe silent running speed in a straight line would be between 10 and 15 knots. However, at the same time we realised that these calculated or estimated limitations could be too theoretical or in the opposite case the incentive of a viable target or the demands of the mission would cause the commander of a submarine to risk his vessel, putting to one side the security measures or exceeding the safe operating limitations.

As for the Carrier Air Wing, it would be firstly used to create an anti-submarine screen using helicopters (coordinated by a destroyer) close to the main body of the group.

There would also be air-search anti-submarine missions based on intelligence reports, assumptions, and previous detections of the enemy. These would be carried out by Tracker aircraft deploying a pattern of sonobuoys in front of the Task Force or along the flank if there were deeper waters where a British submarine could possibly be operating. These sonobuoys would be placed at considerable distance

Destroyer D1 ARA *Hercules* in a rough sea. An Alouette III helicopter is on the flight deck. (www.histarmar.com)

From left to right: *Capitán de Navío* (Retired) Héctor Skare, *Contralmirante* (Retired) Carlos Cal and author Mariano Sciaroni, examining HMS *Splendid´s* Report of Proceedings. Enrique Fortini´s house, 2009. (Enrique Fortini)

from the Task Force, hoping to detect the repositioning of the enemy unit.

As recalled by Héctor Skare, commander of the Anti-Submarine Naval Air Squadron:

> The anti-submarine protection of *25 de Mayo* followed the procedures as laid out in the doctrine: 1) long and short leg zig-zags 2) an anti-submarine screen and lastly 3) anti-submarine searches. The H-3 Sea Kings took part in the second activity in conjunction with the destroyers, although their better use would have been the exploitation of contacts obtained from other methods, amongst these being the S-2Es and occasionally a good radar contact by one of the surface units. We, in the Tracker, made up the essential component of the third activity.
>
> Due to the long-range of our Jezebel sonobuoys, they could easily suffer from interferences from noise generated by our own units. Therefore, we generally kept a great distance, typically 100 nautical miles, between the sonobuoys and the vessels.

Likewise, as much for the surface units as for the aircraft that operated around the aircraft carrier, there was a sonar silence order (in other words the use of active sonar was not authorized, only the passive mode) within a radius of 100 nautical miles of the main body. This was in order not to alert enemy submarines to their presence.

The idea of using only passive sonar was the result of the planning from a team within *Contraalmirante* Allara's headquarters, in face of opposition from other higher-ranking officers who did not wish to depart from the current doctrine. They insisted that an anti-submarine screen be maintained to 21,000 yards from the main body with different surface units, all using their active sonar. This doctrine would be impossible to follow with the resources available, confronted with the speed of a nuclear-powered submarine. There were not sufficient ships (not least with suitable sonar) to protect the high value unit of the formation while, on the other hand, the only thing that the use of active sonar would achieve was to alert the enemy submarine.

The argument over whether to use active sonar angered the junior officers, and at this point it is worth considering the psychology of the naval officers during such discussions. The senior officers did not want to adapt the doctrine, considering this would compromise them in the case of a sinking taking place and not trusting the ability to be able to avoid this eventuality. The more junior officers wanted to develop tactics using passive sonar, but for a completely different reason: they considered that this change in tactics would give them a better possibility of locating an enemy submarine. The more experienced officers in command of the surface units were not at all interested in hunting anybody. Their overriding priority was to avoid becoming prey to a hunting submarine.

It is possible to see this in the report by Allara:

> the analysis carried out in my headquarters about how to operate the sonar equipment during a search phase indicated that it would be best to operate in the passive mode, supported by the following reasons and with a sense of a compromise solution: reduced detection range of active sonar; greater predicted range using listening hydrophones, especially nuclear-powered submarines travelling at high speeds; reduction in acoustic indiscretion of the Task Force by not adding the sound produced by the emission of active sonar.

This was also commented on by ARA *Hércules* Operations Officer, *Capitán de Corbeta* Guillermo Delamer:

> Amongst the measures taken, one was sailing in sonar silence. I believe that this helped us to evade the submarines that were looking for us…If we had been transmitting with our active sonar, I am convinced that we would have ended up with the same fate as the *General Belgrano.*

Lastly, a strict plan of emissions control (EMCON) was elaborated. Any transmission, be it radio or radar, could be detected by specialist equipment, giving the adversary information about the location and characteristics of the emitting unit. Therefore, an order was given limiting the use of any such equipment that could electronically compromise the position of the fleet. These measures were strictly carried out.

To summarise, the generic anti-submarine doctrine supplied by the US Navy (that had undergone its own learning process during the war in the Pacific and the North Atlantic) had been adopted by the Argentine Navy. However, this did not provide solutions in a war fought against nuclear-powered submarines, which had never been imagined as possible adversaries. It had been necessary to adapt that which had been adopted. Therefore, the Task Force 79 finally used an ad-hoc anti-submarine doctrine, one that had never before been put into practice by the Argentine Navy, for the protection of the aircraft carrier.

On the other hand, it is interesting to ask what would have happened had a submarine been detected close to the fleet. As will be seen later, and except for the 3 May incident, these procedures were not carried out in full.

In theory, if a possible submarine was detected, the fleet had to do the following, part of the Integrated ASW Plan:

- The unit that had detected the contact should maintain a prudent distance from it.
- The Tactical Control Officer would launch a Sea King helicopter that would be on alert on the aircraft carrier (there would be one at five minutes alert and another at 30, as well as the Lynx helicopter on board ARA *Santísima Trinidad*) and carry out a vectored attack (VECTAC) towards the contact.
- The rest of the ships in the Task Force would make an emergency turn.
- With this turn a violent zig-zag would be carried out at maximum speed.

It could be said that it was optimistic to think that a nuclear submarine could be kept at bay with only a helicopter.

And now, what did the submarine threat consist of?

4
BRITISH NAVAL STRATEGY IN THE SOUTH ATLANTIC

It is possible to distinguish four different phases of British strategy during the conflict in the South Atlantic, particularly regarding Task Force 324 (submarines).

First, it must be said there were five (of the seven-nuclear-powered hunter-killer submarines available in the Royal Navy) involved in the conflict. These submarines were:

- HMS *Conqueror* and
- HMS *Courageous* (both Churchill class)
- HMS *Valiant* (Valiant class)
- HMS *Splendid* and
- HMS *Spartan* (both being members of the modern Swiftsure class)

These boats were "hunter-killer": designed specifically for attacking other submarines or surface vessels, not to be confused with ballistic missile submarines, that carried nuclear tipped missiles. According to information given out in the British Parliament (which should be attributed a certain level of credibility), no submarine of the latter type modified its patrol or operations during the Falklands/Malvinas conflict, nor were their missiles reprogrammed to engage targets in mainland Argentina.

Likewise, officially only one conventional submarine (diesel-electric) participated in the conflict:

- HMS *Onyx* (Oberon Class)

Summarizing and according to order of appearance in the Theatre of Operations (see table below):

Some rumours indicate that other Oberon-class submarines took part in the conflict, even though this has never been recognized by official sources.

Name	Propulsion	Class	Accepted into service	Displacement submerged (Ton)	Weapons carried during the war	Entering War zone / Leaving
HMS *Spartan*	Nuclear	Swiftsure	1979	4,900	Mk 8 mod 4 / Tigerfish mod. 0	11 April / 9 June
HMS *Splendid*	Nuclear	Swiftsure	1981	4,900	Mk 8 mod 4 / Tigerfish mod. 0	14 April / 28 May
HMS *Conqueror*	Nuclear	Churchill	1971	4,900	Mk 8 mod 4 / Tigerfish mod. 1	16 April / After end of conflict
HMS *Valiant*	Nuclear	Valiant	1966	4,900	Mk 8 mod 4 / Tigerfish mod. 1	15 May / After end of conflict
HMS *Courageous*	Nuclear	Churchill	1971	4,900	Mk 8 mod 4 / Tigerfish mod. 1 / RN Sub Harpoon	28 May / After end of conflict
HMS *Onyx*	Diesel-Electric	Oberon	1967	2,410	Mk 8 mod 4 / Tigerfish mod. 1 / Mk 20S	30 May / After end of conflict

HMS *Conqueror* at Gare Loch at the beginning of the 1980s. (Alistar Lloyd)

HMS *Courageous* in the mid-1980s. (Royal Navy)

The participation of the British submarines can be divided into four phases.

The first phase involved the creation of a Maritime Exclusion Zone (MEZ). It should be remembered that there was no British warship with a reasonable offensive capacity operating in the area, so this was a task left for the submarines to enforce. This started with the arrival of HMS *Spartan*, which had orders to attack Argentine warships or auxiliaries within the zone, which extended on a radius of 200 miles from the centre of the islands. Outside this area, the British submarines were only permitted to attack Argentine shipping as a matter of self-defence.

With the arrival of the surface group in the area, on the 1st May, this same MEZ was declared to be a Total Exclusion Zone (TEZ), which now also threatened Argentine aircraft, including civilian ones carrying out reconnaissance missions inside the same radius. Regarding shipping, it was extended to whatever type of ship, not just Argentine warships and auxiliaries, which might try to break the blockade.

In this second phase, the British stopped carrying out sea denial and moved towards establishing sea control, with the aim of making an amphibious assault on the islands a possibility. The British submarine force, in this stage, reorganised its positioning to optimise the hunt for Argentine surface vessels that could hinder any planned landings.

At first it was not intended to change the Rules of Engagement then in force, except for the authorisation to attack any conventional submarine (which would be presumed to be Argentine).

HMS *Onyx* returning from the war. Note the Jolly Roger flag with a dagger on it. (Royal Navy)

However, shortly thereafter two modifications to the Rules of Engagement were made. The first, taken in a hurry on the afternoon of 30 April, authorised a submarine attack on the carrier *25 de Mayo* outside of the Total Exclusion Zone, except within Argentine territorial waters to the north of parallel 35° W and the 48° S meridian.

The later, taken on 2 May, authorised an attack on any Argentine warships outside the Total Exclusion Zone, with the same restrictions as for the aircraft carrier. This decision was taken secretly, in a hurry just before midnight, to permit the sinking of the *General Belgrano*, being based on intelligence that this old ship formed part of the planned coordinated attack on the Task Force.

Likewise, on 7 May the Total Exclusion Zone was extended up to the Argentine 12-mile territorial limit, something that was already in effect following the sinking of the cruiser. It was important, during this phase, to sink the aircraft carrier. Their mere presence, it was thought, threatened the amphibious force and made possible landings infeasible.

The third phase was the one that corresponds to the landings themselves and the protection of the beachhead. These landings commenced on 21 May in San Carlos and lasted for four days. During this time, with the British fleet relatively committed, some of the most important aerial attacks were carried out by Argentine strike aircraft.

HMS *Conqueror* returning to her home port from the war. (Royal Navy)

The final stage was a response to the requirement to support the land-based operations and was therefore to protect the lines of maritime communication that provided the logistic support to these operations. This took place from 26 May until the end of the conflict.

In these last two phases, and coherent with the requirements of the high command, the British nuclear-powered submarines stopped making offensive patrols and were positioned at key points off the Argentine coast from where they could detect the take-off of aircraft, and in this way, were able to provide the British fleet with a degree of early warning of attacks. Also, they could control the Argentine fleet, which remained in territorial waters, from there.

Obviously, this was not an easy task for the British submariners. Their training and doctrine had qualified them principally to fight against Soviet nuclear submarines (there is nothing better to combat a submarine than another one) in the North Atlantic, the Barents Sea, Norwegian waters and sometimes the Mediterranean.

They had little training in how to deal with the ships and submarines of the Argentines and less so in the waters of the southern hemisphere. As the commander of HMS *Splendid* commented:

> If we had fought against the Russians, I wouldn't have been so bothered as we already knew all about them. However, I did not have any idea about the capabilities of the Argentines.

In fact, if it had not been for the deployment of HMS *Dreadnought* to the islands in 1977 (as part of the small task force sent by the UK to scare off the Argentines when they threatened the islands then) and the information collated by their sonar team during this time, they would have known absolutely nothing about the conditions of the waters around the Falklands/Malvinas.

In this aspect, it's worth praising the ability of the British submariners to adapt – at the time – possibly the best trained in the world. It must be borne in mind that the Argentine Navy was fighting against an elite force.

5
3 MAY – HEADING NORTH

Motivated by the submarine film '*Das Boot*', some of the crew of ARA *Santísima Trinidad* had learned the song '*Tipperary*', which they sang to themselves quite regularly. Following one submarine alarm, they were ordered to stop singing it: "The fools got that one wrong. They enemy would have heard us singing and assumed we were also the Royal Navy" (a crew member from ARA *Santísima Trinidad*).

The 3rd May dawned with cloud cover and some rainfall. The Task Force was heading south-west and trying to stay, as dictated by their orders, in waters with a depth of less than 400 feet. It was a boring morning, adequate to relax from the tensions of the previous days.

During the middle of the morning coffee rounds, at 0842 hrs, the Electronic Warfare Officer on board *Santísima Trinidad* briefly picked up, on his ESM equipment, an intermittent electronic signal (of a type that a submarine's radar might emit). He informed his superior, but he thought that it might have been a spurious contact.

Two hours later, at exactly 1043 hrs, a small radar contact was picked up at a position of 48° 38´S, 65° 36'W. This was approximately 30 miles from Isla Rasa and some 25 miles from the position of the Argentine Task Force. The contact was lost after ten revolutions of the radar antenna.

Now having had two possible contacts, it was decided almost immediately to send a Sea King helicopter to investigate. 2-H-234 took off at 1103 hrs under the command of *Teniente de Navío* Osvaldo Iglesias with *Teniente de Navío* Guillermo Iglesias as co-pilot (nicknamed "Tarzan" and "Oaki" respectively). The rest of the crew of the helicopter was made up by the NCOs Antonio Carbone, Raúl Llanos and Julio Perea.

They arrived at the datum (in other words, the location where the contact on the radar was lost) at 1120 hrs. Iglesias's helicopter transitioned rapidly into a hover, descended, and hovered at a height of 30 feet above the surface of the sea. The sonar operator flicked the switch on his console, and the sonar transducer began to be lowered from beneath the helicopter. At first it oscillated in the air and then entered the water. In an area of such shallow water, the sonar operator didn't have to wait long to stop lowering the transducer. He then started listening carefully to the sounds in his headphones and analysing the signal on the console in front of him. However, he could only make out marine life noises.

With the sonar once again out of the water, "Tarzan" gained a little height and accelerated the heavy machine to a new location in the Argentine Sea, some 12 nautical miles to the south-east of their initial contact point. With this second dip of the sonar, the operator was surprised to hear the ping of an active sonar on an approximate bearing of between 330° and 030°. This sound, of course, could not have come from a natural source, even though this contact didn't give any idea of distance or the characteristics of the emitter. Once more they retrieved the transducer and moved to a new position to the north.

The tension only increased when the third dip of the sonar produced a mechanical noise on the hydrophone at about 110°. Unfortunately, this contact rapidly weakened and could not be regained. The anti-submarine task finished at 1256 hrs when the helicopter was almost at the limit of its endurance. They had been close, but very alone on the search.

With a retrospective analysis, the impression remains that this anti-submarine effort was insufficient, seeing as there had been ESM, radar and sonar contact with a man-made object near to the fleet. It is possible for this reason, that in the future more assets would be deployed if a contact was established, so that any uncertainty could be classified.

It was evident, within the Argentine Task Force that the hunt had begun. With this contact, it was clear for everyone that there was a submarine operating in the area.

The Argentine sailors started getting impatient, nerves began to get a bit frayed and questions about what would happen if their ship was hit by a torpedo were asked. It's worth remembering *Belgrano* had been torpedoed just the day before.

Regarding the feelings about the submarine menace, *Teniente de Navío* 'Quique' Fortini, a Tracker pilot embarked on the carrier, recalls:

As I saw it, there seemed to be two different sensations. First there were some, like us – anti-submariners – that evaluated professionally the threat of a torpedo. The rest, the majority on board, who initially hadn't thought too much about the subject until the *Belgrano* was sunk. From that moment, they then over-thought the subject before settling on a more stable position.

For example, some officers stopped using the bathrooms in the aircraft carrier as they had tiled floors. They had considered, with good sense, that in the event of an explosion these tiles would fragment into shrapnel.

Other crew members started to wear life vests when resting, or changed where they were sleeping, as described by *Cabo Segundo* Francisco 'Pancho' Kawa, a crewman on ARA *Santísima Trinidad*:

SP-2H Neptune (2-P-112), one of the two serviceable Neptunes available to the *Comando de Aviación Naval,* located the British Task Force on 4 May, which enabled the mounting of the Exocet attack that struck HMS *Sheffield* that same day. HMS *Sheffield* sank a few days later whilst being towed to South Georgia by HMS *Yarmouth.* (*Armada Argentina*)

> Until the sinking of the *Belgrano*, all activity on board was carried out 'according to the book'. From that point going forward, you started to see situations from a little unhappiness through to extreme precautions.
>
> Some began to move their mattresses to places close to their action stations posts, mostly to the upper decks close to the radar area using the pretext that they wanted to be closer to their action station in case of an alarm, even sleeping in the corner of their posts and only leaving to eat or to go to the toilet, even being pushed out by others with shouts of *"go bathe yourself dirty so and so, and then come back!"*

Aside from these anecdotes, there were no instances of blind panic. Every man managed to address their fear and channel it to their own personal benefit, and that of the navy. A Sea King pilot remembers:

> We managed to live with the threat posed by the submarines better than I had imagined. I think this happened because we had confidence in our own capacity and what each one of us had to do. (Oscar Brandeburgo)

Amongst the younger crew members, the attitude was the same:

> You could say that amongst the younger sailors there was an excessive confidence, or irresponsibility, a product of various factors such as youth (I had just turned 19), high morale, and that we were finally going to put what we had learned into practice; adrenaline was at a maximum and it didn't matter if the threat was a submarine, ship or aircraft. Quoting from Julius Caesar, *"Alea iacta est"*. (Francisco Kawa)

Further to the south of the position of Task Force 79.1, the Argentine Navy were investigating another possible submarine contact. There is a mistaken idea that nuclear-powered submarines will always stay submerged in deep water, and never come up near the surface and expose its masts. This is just not true, as a nuclear-powered submarine will sail submerged just beneath the waves with its masts and antennas raised above the surface a lot more than has commonly been written about. Therefore, it is not unreasonable to suppose that one can be detected by radar or visually.

At 0615 hrs, an aircraft had taken off from the naval air base at Rio Grande, on the coast of Tierra del Fuego, under the command of *Capitán de Corbeta* Julio H. Pérez Roca with *Teniente de Navío* Luís Guillermo "Bichi" Arbini seated to his right as co-pilot.

This aircraft was one of the worn-out SP-2H Neptunes, bearing the registration 2-P-111, that belonged to the Reconnaissance Naval Air Squadron (*Escuadrilla Aeronaval de Exploración*). It had taken off on a search mission to look for survivors from the *General Belgrano* sinking. Its main mission was a surface search; however, its crew were trained in anti-submarine warfare and it was carrying a standard load of sonobuoys and torpedoes.

The Neptunes had already had an earlier encounter with submarines. Just before midday on 16 April, the same aircraft, piloted on this occasion by *Capitán de Corbeta* Julio E. Kalauz, while it was carrying out a training exercise with aircraft of the Argentine Air Force, picked up a small radar contact some 60 miles to the north of the Falklands/Malvinas. This was inside the Maritime Exclusion Zone.

Overcoming their initial shock, the commander of the aircraft decided to investigate it. When sonobuoys were dropped, they picked up the acoustic signature of a high-speed turbine and *Teniente de Corbeta* José A. Andersen, the Tactical Coordinator, evaluated this as belonging to a nuclear-powered submarine. Unfortunately, on this occasion, the aircraft was not carrying any homing torpedoes. They were ordered, from land, to ignore the contact and to continue with the joint-exercise to guide the Air Force attack aircraft participating in the exercise. These included Canberras from Trelew, A-4s from Rio Gallegos and San Julián, Mirages from Comodoro Rivadavia and Daggers from Rio Grande.

It has never been possible to determine which submarine had been detected. But a few days previously the Uruguayan Air Force had reported a possible Soviet submarine in transit towards the south, on a course consistent with this contact.

Returning to 2-P-111 on 3 May, whilst it was searching for life-rafts from the sunk *Belgrano*, at 0930 hrs the lookout in the bow of the aircraft sighted what he understood were the masts of a submarine at 56° 00'S, 59° 30'W. This was reported to the ships operating in the area, and the aircraft was ordered to dedicate itself to the pursuit of this contact, launching passive sonobuoys over it.

But, after a couple of hours of fruitless work, and due to the lack of other reconnaissance aircraft, the Navy command ordered that the Neptune finish the quest for the supposed submarine and return to its previous mission of searching for the cruiser's life-rafts, which it did a short time later.

The obligatory question is whether this sighting was submarine HMS *Conqueror* (which was understood to be operating in this area), a whale, or just an optical illusion. HMS *Conqueror* (S48) is perhaps the most famous of the British submarines that took part in the Falklands/Malvinas conflict.

It was under the command of Commander Chris Wreford-Brown, a graduate of the Royal Navy's 'Perisher' course (the command course for submarine officers), the equivalent of a PhD in submarine warfare. He was 35 years old in 1982, the same age as his peers in *Splendid*, *Spartan* and *Onyx* (also 'Perisher' graduates). Although Wreford-Brown had taken command of *Conqueror* just three weeks before the start of the crisis, he was already very experienced in underwater warfare.

Conqueror was a nuclear-powered attack submarine of the Churchill class, with a submerged displacement of 4,900 tonnes, which served in the Royal Navy between 1971 and 1990. Its principle role was one of anti-submarine and anti-surface warfare, focused on the threat of the Soviet Navy, which was at the time of its construction, gaining ever greater ocean-going capability.

It had a maximum submerged speed of 26 knots, bearing in mind that the towed array (a very efficient sonar at the end of a cable towed behind a submarine, away from the boat's own noise sources) caused it to lose a knot of its original speed. Its endurance, like all nuclear-powered submarines, was limited only by the requirements of food for the crew that operated it.

It had six torpedo tubes in the bow, which were capable of firing either Mk 24 Tigerfish Mod. 1 homing torpedoes (with a dual anti-submarine and anti-surface role) as well as the older Mk 8 straight-run torpedoes. However, the Tigerfish that it carried was an early version that had various short-comings as an anti-surface weapon, as it had been developed primarily as an anti-submarine weapon.

These problems were still concurrent in 1982, which was borne out by the fact that HMS *Onyx* later would have difficulty sinking the burned-out hulk of LSL *Sir Galahad*, sunk as a war grave, with this weapon. *Onyx* attempted to fire two Tigerfish, neither of which left the torpedo tubes. They finally had to close to 1,500 yards distance from the charred remains of *Galahad* and use a Mk 8 to send it to its final resting place in the depths of the South Atlantic[1]. The Tigerfish had design flaws in the guidance system, the batteries and the warhead itself. These deficiencies were only finally overcome in 1988.

In his post war Report of Proceedings, Admiral Herbert (FOSM) wrote about this torpedo:

> It was rejected in favour of the Mk 8 for use against BELGRANO because of its unproven lethality, know unreliability and the relative small punch of the warhead when used against a cruiser with armoured strengthening on its hull.

To attack surface targets, therefore, the venerable Mk 8 (with a design that has its origins in 1925) was the preferred torpedo. The strange situation was that most of the British submarine commanders preferred to use the antiquated straight-run torpedoes, whose optimal parameters of fire required the position of the submarine to be 1,200 yards from the target at an angle of 90°, to the more modern Tigerfish which had a range of 23,000 yards and which could move intelligently. With this in mind, the commander of *Conqueror* had noted down in his war diary that he would use the Mk 8s in most scenarios except if he did not have a perfect firing solution.

The involvement of *Conqueror* in the Falklands/Malvinas War had started when the submarine left its home base of Faslane (Scotland) on 4 April, following the embarkation of 12 members of the SBS (Special Boat Service). Its transit to the zone of operations was made close to its maximum speed (at an average of 22 knots), straining the submarine's engines in the extreme. As remembered by the Navigation Officer, Jonathon 'Jonty' Powis, who would retire from the Royal Navy with the rank of Commander:

> The submarine must have woken every sonar operator in the Atlantic; she had two un-insulated turbo-driven feed pumps for the full power state, which screamed.

By the 16th April it arrived in the area of operations and four days later it suffered damage to its communications aerial, as recounted by the Navigation Officer:

> Earlier we had suffered a minor bump possibly with some ice that had damaged our VHF aerial, and so we lost SSIXS (Submarine Satellite Information Exchange Sub-System – the submarine's satellite-based communications system). We were also operating far outside the design coverage of NATO VLF stations. Thus, communications had become a problem.

This problem was overcome to some extent with some ingenuity on the part of the crew. A few days later it took part in the retaking of South Georgia, circumnavigating the island carrying out visual and electronic searches. In those waters it took part in the search for the submarine ARA *Santa Fe.*

The *Santa Fe*, under the command of *Capitán de Corbeta* Horacio Bicain, had been ordered to take a patrol position on 23 April some 70 miles to the west of South Georgia. It was there that it was detected on *Conqueror's* passive sonar whilst snorkelling. Calculating that it was close by, Wreford-Brown ordered the periscope to be raised so he could carry out a visual search. Unable to detect the submarine visually, the British submarine returned to the depths, assuming the *Santa Fe* had finished charging its batteries and had dived once again.

It was unable to regain contact. The Argentine vessel had slipped away on the surface, at full speed, away from *Conqueror's* hunting zone. Unfortunately for the *Santa Fe,* it was located later while still sailing on the surface and was damaged by Royal Navy helicopters. *Santa Fe* was finally captured in South Georgia.

From 28 April, *Conqueror* was repositioned to operate between the Falkland Islands and Isla de los Estados, which is where it hunted down and sank *General Belgrano* on 2 May. Following the attack, it

Submarine S-21 ARA *Santa Fe* (ex-USS *Catfish*) near its home port of *Mar del Plata*, 400 km to the south of Buenos Aires. *Santa Fe* was captured by British forces in late April 1982. (www.histarmar.com)

detected ships sent to help with the rescue of the crew of the *Belgrano* several times, but had orders not to attack any ships that were carrying out this humanitarian mission.

Likewise, it was ordered to protect HMS *Sheffield*, which had been badly damaged following the Exocet missile attack carried out by the Argentine Naval Aviation, against any possible missile attack by surface units. This mission was later cancelled when it was determined that HMS *Sheffield* was a write-off. Curiously, a contrary order was given to the commander of the Argentine submarine ARA *San Luis* by the Argentine Submarine Command: this was to sink the damaged destroyer. Similarly, this order was rescinded once it became clear the ship was damaged beyond use.

HMS *Conqueror's* anti-surface patrol to the south and south-east of the Falklands/Malvinas finished on 5 May, when the submarine was assigned a sea denial mission within the Total Exclusion Zone.

During that period, her Officer of the Watch thought that it had been spotted by a Neptune aircraft: while navigating with some of its masts exposed on the surface, some 100 miles to the west of the Falklands/Malvinas, a low-flying aircraft was observed and two minutes later a noise similar to a torpedo being dropped in the water was detected. This triggered the submarine to begin evasive manoeuvres and to move away from the area at maximum speed[2].

The Neptunes were not operating that day and the aircraft that was detected was probably C-130 Hercules TC-68 of the Argentine Air Force, returning to the mainland after a successful logistics run to the islands and unaware of the commotion it had caused in the waters below.

Later, on 23 May, some dangerous repairs were carried out on the surface because an aerial wire had become entangled in the propeller. For this repair, Petty Officer Graham 'Horse' Libby was awarded the George Medal[3].

It is also interesting to note that during the first days of June *Conqueror* was given the order to sink the destroyer ARA *Hércules*. Trying to fulfil this mission the submarine entered Golfo San Matías and managed to operate in waters of less than 160 feet depth.

Other tasks it carried out included providing protection to logistics convoys sailing between Ascension Island and the Falklands/Malvinas and, from the beginning of June it carried out reconnaissance of the Argentine coast and reported any air activity.

Conqueror returned to its home port flying the traditional skull and cross-bones black and white flag, known as the 'Jolly Roger', for the sinking of the cruiser. This flag also had a small dagger on it, which implied that it had participated in a commando mission.

Now, going back to 3 May, *Conqueror* was close to the general area being patrolled by 2-P-111. Even though the submarine didn't make visual contact of the aircraft, it had been detected by its ESM equipment and correctly classified as a Neptune. In its war diary, the commander wrote: *"I would imagine the Neptune rackets are aircraft searching for me around the datum area."*

However, *Conqueror* was located some 150 nautical miles to the west and moving away from the datum being searched by the Argentine Navy's aircraft. Therefore, it could not have been this submarine. Consequently, the result should be adjusted to read "NONSUB". After analysis, the Neptune crew concluded the same.

It is not surprising at the end of that day that *Conqueror's* CO wrote the following in the war diary: "Neptunes have been active all day searching for me, but I have been outside their search area. A quiet day after yesterday!"

This alarm was the first of many that would occur in the days ahead. This happened because the British submarines did expose themselves to possible detection on a regular basis. For example, HMS *Splendid* (and applying this routine to its submarine sisters), between 3 and 8 May exposed its masts or sailed just beneath the surface to trail its communications cable every four hours, on average, to receive radio

An Argentine Air Force C-130 Hercules landing at Puerto Argentino/Port Stanley Airport, on April 1982. Hercules TC-68, callsign "*Pato*" (Duck), was most probably the airplane sighted by HMS *Conqueror* on 7 May. (*Fuerza Aérea Argentina*)

traffic, make visual searches or send situation reports.

The satellite bandwidth (and therefore the speed of transmission and reception of data) cannot have been very satisfactory as, according to their war diary, they it would take between 20 and 30 minutes to send or receive radio messages. This, of course, increased the possibility of the submarine being detected.

The reason for the frequent exposure of the masts of the submarines can be explained with three factors. In the first place, the lack of knowledge of the Argentine ships possessed by the sonar operators and the need to adequately identify targets required the commander, prior to taking any kind of offensive activity (and according to the Rules of Engagement), to try to make a visual identification.

In the second place, it must be considered that communication coverage was lacking (remembering that the operations were being carried out outside the usual NATO areas).

Finally, the Headquarters in Northwood had established an overwhelming radio routine requiring the subordinate commanders to send constant situation reports. This is better explained in the words of the commander of HMS *Splendid*:

> The obsession with information, feedback from the fleet to keep the politicians happy...but what happened here is we got into the old-fashioned surface way of doing things of sending SITREPS (Situation Reports). So, we were being forced to send SITREPS when I didn't want to send them…I sent 103 situation SITREPS during the Falklands war. As far as I am concerned, that's 102 more than I should have done.... A submarine is designed to keep quiet.

There was no doubt, therefore, that the British submarines remained a part of the conflict either with their masts up and trailing their communication aerials just below the surface, or in some cases on the surface of the sea.

Likewise, it should not be forgotten that a submarine, even a nuclear-powered one, will be unaware of the fact that it is being hunted until its equipment detects the unmistakable sounds of high-revolution propellers and active sonar emissions of the type used by homing torpedoes.

This must be born in mind to interpret correctly the actions that happened further north in the following days.

6
4 MAY – A TENSE WAIT

> As the distance shortened it was possible to work out the disposition of the enemy with more clarity, but the appearance of aircraft accompanying the ships complicated everything. The Trackers and helicopters from 25 de Mayo were moving from one side to the other forcing me to use the periscope very cautiously, but I felt compelled to expose it briefly every three to four minutes. With each sweep of the periscope I tried to locate the troublesome Sea Kings and Trackers. The formers were moving from one location to another, each time dipping its sonar when they came to a hover, and the Trackers were searching wide areas with their electronic and magnetic search capability as well as visually. By doing this, and managing to avoid detection and furtively observing the surface activity we closed in on their surface force, although it's probably more appropriate to say that it was closing in on us. ("*Submarinos. Su historia, relatos y curiosidades*" by Roberto L Pertusio)

In the pre-flight room, or pilot's ready-room, on board *25 de Mayo* a sensation of a tense wait prevailed.

Located in the bowels of the ship and shared by all the embarked squadrons, it consisted of two areas divided by a screen, with seating for some twenty pilots. It was also equipped with a television, not for watching sports news but which allowed all the landings on the flight deck to be observed. It also contained a refrigerator, which was always fully stocked and would regularly be raided by the hungry anti-submarine aircrews that had just returned from long over-water missions. The responsibility to keep it full fell to the crew of the aircraft carrier, and this sometimes led to some jealousies and disagreements. The members of the Carrier Air Wing simply shrugged their shoulders and argued that it was impossible to fly with empty stomachs.

In the front rows were the three Tracker crews that were tasked to fly the immediately upcoming sorties. Immediately behind them sat the rest of the squadron. At the back were other colleagues and unrelated members of the crew that had no need to be there, but didn't bother anyone nevertheless.

The detection of a submarine the previous day had cause a substantial change of mood. The crews that were to fly missions would listen and take note of things necessary and pertinent to the mission. These missions would have been planned jointly, as explained by the Operations Officer of the carrier:

> With reference to the planning of anti-submarine operations it's necessary to make a small introduction. The airborne anti-submarine warfare capability in Argentina changed radically with the arrival of the S-2E Trackers and the subsequent development of the use of the Jezebel sonobuoys by the Anti-Submarine Naval Air Squadron. This development was gradual and was enlarged and improved year by year, but its diffusion to the rest of the Navy was slower. Back then, in 1982, the naval personnel with the most knowledge of modern anti-submarine warfare were the command core of this squadron. Without wishing to diminish the authority of those higher up the command chain, in those days the squadron leadership were better prepared than those in higher levels. Doctrine dictated that the tactics to be developed were planned by the Operations Department of the Task Force and selected by the Commander. However, the tactics were drawn up in close coordination with the squadron and on many occasions completely from within the squadron itself. It is worth considering that there were only a few metres of separation between the people involved (a ship is a very small space) and who had daily dealings with each other, as well as many years of shared tasks and responsibility, therefore the planning was very agile and through constant consultations.

Once the pre-flight briefings were over, some aircrew headed straight for the refrigerator, others directly to the flight deck.

Unbeknownst to the Argentine sailors, the Royal Navy HQ in Northwood had just sent a new flash message to its nuclear-powered submarines in the South Atlantic, reminding them that while it was permitted to attack any enemy vessel (within the limitations set out by the current Rules of Engagement) *25 de Mayo* was still right at the top of the list of priority targets. This message was taken very seriously on board *Splendid*.

The nuclear-powered attack submarine HMS *Splendid* (S106), under the command of Commander Roger Lane-Nott, was a Swiftsure Class boat that served in the Royal Navy between 1979 and 2004. It had a submerged displacement of 4,900 tonnes and was capable of a sustained maximum speed of a little over 30 knots. Its armament comprised of five forward torpedo tubes which were capable of firing both straight-run and intelligent torpedoes. Later, following the conflict, the class acquired the capacity to launch Harpoon anti-ship missiles and Tomahawk cruise missiles.

At the outbreak of the crisis, it found herself in the North Atlantic, furtively following a Soviet Victor class hunter-killer submarine, when a communication that had started out as routine suddenly ordered it to return to port early and to prepare for a possible deployment as a response to the unfolding events in the Falklands/Malvinas.

After restocking in Faslane, it headed south on the 1st April (the day before the Argentine attack) and two weeks later, after a long high-speed run (it sailed at an average speed of 23.8 knots) found itself on station near the Islands.

On arrival, it was assigned a patrol area to the north east of the Maritime Exclusion Zone, the closest one to the continent. For some days *Splendid* patrolled this area, also being sent off to reconnoitre various points and ports, and finally ended up patrolling around the mouth of the Rio de la Plata (in the Buenos Aires Province). According to its CO:

> I spent quite a lot of time, basically up-threat, to try to intercept anything that was between the Falklands and Argentina…their main bases. I spent time both in front of places such as Comodoro Rivadavia, Gallegos and up to the River Plate.

On 21 April, British intelligence services had pinpointed the location of the Argentine aircraft carrier around 90 nautical miles from Punta Delgada (in the Chubut Province) and about 480 miles from the islands. The submarine was ordered to head to this area and try to locate the ship with a view to the eventual initiation of offensive actions. *25 de Mayo* was located on the 23rd, sailing south just a few miles from the coast, which made its destruction impossible given the Rules of Engagement in force at the time. Frustratingly, contact with the carrier was lost a short time later.

On the 26th, *Splendid*, while level with Comodoro Rivadavia, spotted the two Type 42 destroyers that belonged to the Argentine Navy. Later, it also detected the three A-69 corvettes and proceeded to follow them as intelligence had suggested that they would be the escorting group to the carrier and would shortly be reunited with it.

> On 26 April I found myself in a situation where I had, in one

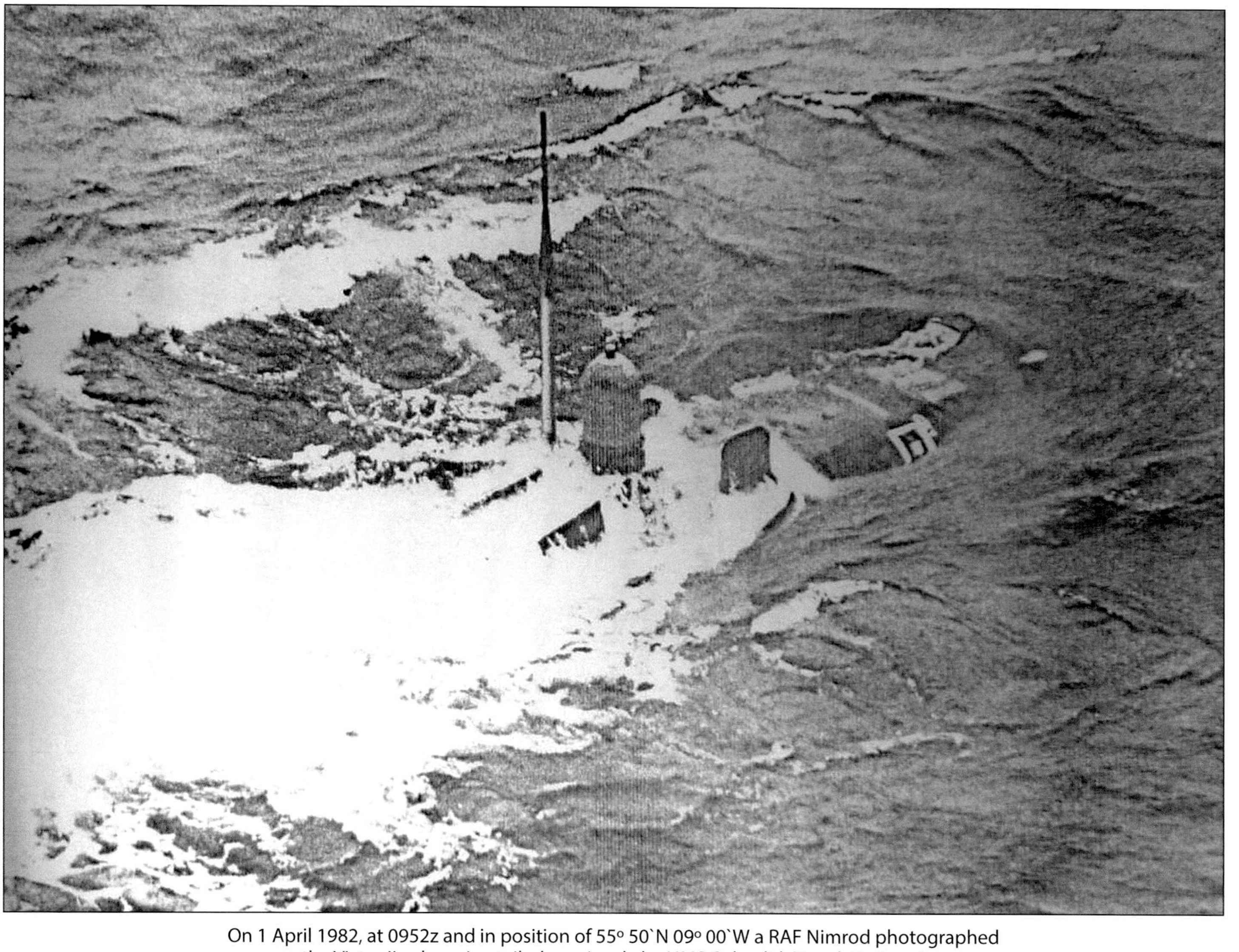

On 1 April 1982, at 0952z and in position of 55º 50`N 09º 00`W a RAF Nimrod photographed the Victor II submarine tailed previously by HMS *Splendid*. (Royal Air Force)

> sweep of the periscope, within 14,000 yards (that's 7 miles)…two Type 42 frigates, identified as Argentine, and three A-69 frigates. So, effectively, I had the total of the escort forces of the Argentine Navy. All outside of the 12-mile limit. All within one sweep of the periscope.

However, just twenty-four hours later the commander of the submarine received an order to break off his pursuit and to head north to a new position that intelligence thought that the elusive *25 de Mayo* would be found.

It didn't make any sense, bearing in mind that the aircraft carrier, out of necessity, would need to meet up with its escorts before entering the open sea. At first, Lane-Nott refused to comply with the new order but had no choice when he was contacted directly by Admiral Herbert (the Flag Officer Submarines) having ignored the order for the whole day.[1]

His frustration was further compounded when they found nothing at the new coordinates and did not regain contact with the Argentine ships until 29 April, specifically the corvettes, and at this point the Commander decided to head south once again in their pursuit. However, some hours later, he had to reduce speed to send a report by radio (which required extending the communications mast at periscope depth – and this would be damaged if the speed of the submarine exceeded around 8 knots), and at that moment the ships accelerated away heading south east: the contact was lost once again. Later that day they also detected the Type 42s and *Py*, but still not their assigned high-value target.

Around midnight on the 1st May, the British intelligence once again located the Argentine aircraft carrier and Northwood HQ transmitted its location to the submarine (and, as previously mentioned, also to *Spartan*). However, they received the signal late and when they arrived at the search area, the flagship of the Argentine fleet was nowhere to be seen. On the 2nd, it had sporadic contacts with the Argentine Task Force, without being able to arrive at an interception point. Despite the efforts of the commander, the Argentine aircraft carrier had managed to escape their grasp on several occasions.

The 3rd had detected an Argentine Navy Sea King, while shadowing the darkened Argentine fleet on a south-east heading. However, they were not able to locate them until the end of the day, as noted in his report of 2059 on 3 May:

> After losing contact with the units at the beginning of the day, we may after a long dash to the south west, have regained contact. We will hang on to it now.

"We will hang on to it now." They hoped that on this 4th they would finally be able to sink one of the Argentine ships, maybe even the aircraft carrier.

One of the messages they received that day also told them about ships of the Argentine Navy to the north east of their position (in fact, although British intelligence didn't know it, they were less than 50 miles away). Lane-Nott must have been grateful once again for the information supplied by Her Majesty's intelligence services.

The information obtained by the British came from various sources. In the first place, the encryption machines being used by the Argentine Navy were of Swiss origin and didn't present much of an obstacle for British or US intelligence services. In effect, the machines manufactured by the Swiss company Crypto AG were apparently no obstacles for the experts at the National Security Agency (NSA) of the United States, who shared their information with their peers at the British GCHQ. Some versions of events, which appeared after the conflict, insinuated that the manufacturer had made some agreements with the biggest western intelligence agencies, which made it easy for them to decipher supposedly secure messages. For this reason, the commercial representative of Crypto AG in Iran was detained in 1992 and only released nine months later, following a commercial and diplomatic scandal.[2]

Further to this, during the interesting debate that took place in the House of Commons on 3 April, Edward Rowlands (the MP for Merthyr Tydfil), who had previously held positions in the Foreign Office, clearly stated that Argentine diplomatic communications, also encrypted using Crypto AG machines, were easily readable: *"I shall make a disclosure. As well as trying to read the mind of the enemy, we have been reading its telegrams for many years."*

The interception of communications made it possible, for example, for Rear Admiral Woodward to know the patrol area of the Argentine

HMS *Splendid* returning to HM Naval Base Clyde, after her involvement in the Iraqi conflict in July 2003. (Royal Navy)

submarine ARA *San Luis* on the 1st May and send a Task Force to locate and destroy it, fortunately (for those on-board the submarine) without success. According to Admiral Herbert:

> GCHQ Cheltenham was by far the most important source of intelligence on Argentine naval forces. Their contribution was invaluable to the success of the submarine campaign.

Traditional spying methods (HUMINT or HUMan INTelligence), carried out mainly by the ever present Chilean spy ring, should also be borne in mind when considering sources of information. The fact that the main Argentine naval bases, such as Mar del Plata, were easily observed from the outside undoubtedly made this task much easier.

The final source of information came courtesy of the United States, in the form of intelligence gathered by its modern low-orbit reconnaissance satellites. In April 1982, the United States had three satellites of this category in orbit, one KH-8 (Project "Gambit-3") and two KH-11 ("Kennan" or "Crystal"). The KH-8 finished its mission on 23 May, being replaced by a KH-9 bird (Project "Hexagon") launched a little earlier, on 11 May.

The United States had diverted KH-11/4 (launched on 3 September 1981) from its normal orbit and had reprogrammed it to make passes over the South Atlantic. These big satellites had a maximum daytime optical resolution of ten centimetres and night-time resolution of 60 centimetres via its radar and infra-red sensors, which is basically the equivalent of the Hubble space telescope pointed towards the Earth instead of the stars. These satellites supplied intelligence in near real time.

Each of the KH-11 satellites was also accompanied by three electronic intelligence satellites which travelled in orbit alongside the mother satellite and could triangulate the position of any radio or electromagnetic source that broke its silence. In other words, the KH-11 could provide an unsurpassed panorama of the conflict zone. However, even satellite imagery could not provide tactical information, because of the delay between the images being transmitted to the ground, processed, analysed and finally turned over to a relevant operational command. Satellite images could be useful to establish if there were ships in port or anchored near the coast[3].

Of greater tactical use, also shared during the war, were the ELINT "White Cloud" satellites operated by the US Navy[4]. These satellites, usually grouped in three, could detect electronic signals in a radius of 1,727 nautical miles.

Certain intelligence was also passed to British intelligence from a Norwegian listening station that was capable of eavesdropping on communications from Soviet maritime reconnaissance satellites equipped with radars (RORSAT) designed to find ships on the high seas.

The submarine threat was therefore multiplied given the excellent quality of intelligence provided to the units down south. This was hardly surprising given that intelligence is one of the fundamental pillars of modern naval warfare.

Returning to the aircraft carrier, the first of the scheduled anti-submarine flights on that 4th May was carried out by Tracker 2-AS-22, which was launched at 0023 hrs under the command of *Teniente de Navío* Juan José *"Lince"* ("Lynx") Membrana with the remainder of the crew made up by *Teniente de Fragata* Gustavo Ottogalli, *Cabo Principal* Paulinkas and *Cabo Primero* Condorí. Their mission was to lay a sonobuoy field at the mouth of the Golfo San Jorge, covering the eastern (and more vulnerable) flank of the Task Force. They took off successfully using the single steam catapult on *25 de Mayo* and once the aircraft arrived at its start point, it started laying the passive barrier.

In all anti-submarine operations carried out by the Trackers, the sonobuoy was the main sensor used for sub-aquatic searches. These were placed with consideration to their range of effective detection, and other factors such as time, place, and meteorological conditions. The effective range was calculated using tables that had been produced by the squadron along with the Naval Hydrographic Service (*Servicio de Hidrografía Naval*). These tables gave the approximate required distance of placement between sonobuoys necessary, so that no submarine could creep past a given point in the Argentine Sea.

Of course, different factors would affect this equation – factors that could not be determined in advance. Therefore, the first Tracker to lay a barrier would communicate the details to an Argentine Naval ground station which would in turn pass this information on to the Naval Hydrographic Service via its land-line. The receiver would update the factors and, in real time, the duty technicians would provide the crew on the aircraft with the predicted range that could be expected on each of the frequencies being used on the sonobuoys that would be deployed (all relayed back to the aircraft using the same communication chain). In this way, the pilot could make the correct decision about the sonobuoys with the knowledge that the task would be carried out with a degree of precision. The average distance between sonobuoys was around eight nautical miles, which was around one and a half times the predicted range of a Jezebel, as indicated in the manuals dedicated to the laying of a passive field.

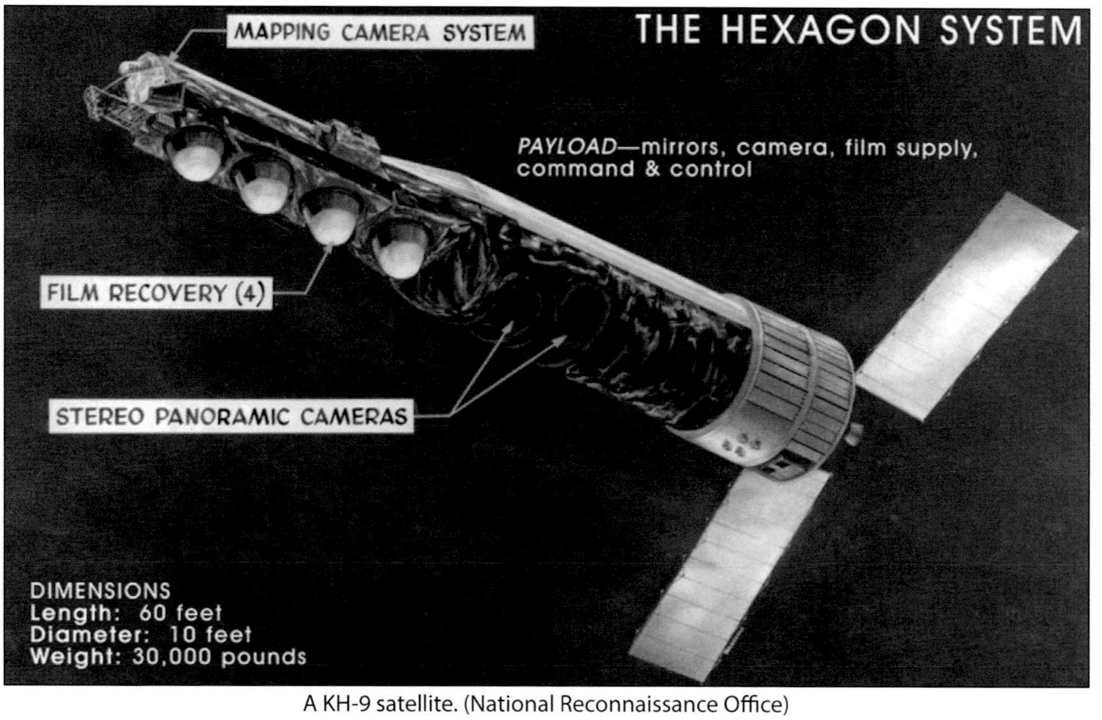

A KH-9 satellite. (National Reconnaissance Office)

Another shot of ARA *25 de Mayo,* this time with a clear flight deck. (*Armada Argentina*)

All this development of anti-submarine warfare in shallow waters had been conceived by the Argentine Navy, which had developed various tables, analyses of sound and propagation at shallow depths, creating physical models and other such things. This was because books, manuals and conferences that came from the pre-eminent naval power in the world (the United States) dealt exclusively with the search for Soviet submarines in deep waters. This was not at all the applicable case for the Argentine Navy. The US Navy only became really interested in what it termed as being "Littoral Warfare", or naval warfare in coastal waters, after the end of the Cold War.

With all these factors in mind, a sonobuoy field would usually consist of between three and eight sonobuoys, with the aircraft overhead orbiting at around 7,000 feet to be able to maintain radio contact with each one of the buoys and to make the detection of the aircraft's engines by a submarine more difficult. This height would also make it possible to carry out sporadic searches with the radar.

Of course, the analysis of the signals coming from the buoys was carried out supposing the presence of a diesel electric conventional submarine, which was the only type the operators had trained in tracking. Obviously, the difference in sounds produced some "holes" in the complex framework of underwater detection, in which a nuclear submarine might have been able to place itself. One of the Tracker's most experienced acoustic operators explained:

> Generally, in the Argentine Navy of the time, the barriers were made up by parallel lines which when deployed together form equilateral triangles where the vertices are made by the position of sonobuoys. This method of forming triangles has a simple effect of making it possible to locate a contact by using more than one of the sonobuoys. This procedure has two important premises. The first is that the contact is a conventional submarine and the second is that the processor on board the Tracker only allows the use of omnidirectional sonobuoys. (Héctor M. Carrizo)

Returning now to *Teniente* Membrana's aircraft, having sown its sonobuoys in accordance with the procedure outlined above, it didn't gain any contacts although the sonar operator did pick up some distant propeller noises, probably those of fishing vessels.

The Tracker crew were of top quality. They could deploy and monitor 13 sonobuoys – something that was not usual and demonstrated their ability to *"go further than normal"*. They obviously could not monitor all of them at the same time (due to the limitations of the AQA-4), but they switched between them every 15 minutes. However, nothing of interest was picked up by them on that night of frustration.

With no contacts gained from the sonobuoys, the commander of the aircraft ordered a change of tactics. Instead of carrying out monotonous orbits, he communicated to the crew that they would begin to carry out a random radar search outside the area covered by the sonobuoys. The idea was to induce a possible contact to modify its behaviour, for example to increase speed or change course; these dynamic changes generated sound, and this in turn could be detected by the sonobuoys.

Exchanging a quick glance with the co-pilot, the commander throttled up the engines and ordered the radar operator start his search and to wait for something to happen. However, the only thing he heard was *"no contacts, sir"*, first from the radar operator and then from the acoustic operator, something that both would continue to repeat over the length of the following minutes. At about then, *Teniente* Membrana told the crew that their hunt that night wasn't going very well. He thought that the nuclear-powered submarine must be in another area. His crew would be better off sleeping soundly, something that made him feel a bit grumpy. However, he was mistaken. Tracker 2-AS-22 had been causing quite a commotion just under the surface of the sea.

At 0240 hrs, the Officer of the Watch on board *Splendid* wanted to come to periscope depth to carry out a visual search and send a situation report. The submarine's sonar had a large contact at some 15 nautical miles and the officer want to know if it was possible to close on it without placing the submarine in danger.

The submarine slowed to a speed of 6 knots, and when the Engineering Officer signalled that the submarine was "balanced" (perfectly equilibrated along its longitudinal axis), the officer in command ordered it to periscope depth.

Inside the submarine everyone was ready to occupy their positions. At 0307 hrs, having already deployed its various antennas, the ESM operator detected an AN/APS-88 radar to the north west. It did not appear to be anything to worry about as it seemed to be some distance away: there was no real danger of the radar waves being transmitted by the aircraft bouncing off the periscope and aerial. With all the time in the world, he proceeded to classify this contact as "E-42" and started to track it.

British submariners would classify contacts with a letter prefix according to the method of contact. An "S" if it was obtained by sonar; "R" if by radar; "V" if visually and an "E" if captured by the ESM equipment. If the contact was gained by two or more sensors it would be given an "M" ("Master") prefix. The number assigned to the contact was unique and consecutive. In this way, for example, "S-21" would be the 21st contact of a patrol in this case obtained by a sonar contact, and "V-23" would be the 23rd contact which had been gained visually. If, following the above examples, contact "S-21" was corroborated by a radar contact, it would be reclassified as "M-21".

An S-2E Tracker about to recover onto the *25 de Mayo* as seen from the Control Tower. (*Armada Argentina*)

On this occasion, the energy being emitted by contact "E-42" was coming from the Tracker being flown by *Teniente de Navío* Membrana. At 0531 hrs, while *Splendid* continued sending and receiving radio communications, the ESM operator noted the radar signal had significantly increased in strength and informed the officer in command the submarine could be detected at any moment. The submarine therefore immediately sought safety at depth, as annotated by its commander: "E-42, a probable Neptune, appears to be searching an area to the north east. We will go deep to keep clear of him, he may be in Area Juan."

This gave a certain advantage to the Argentine fleet since the abrupt change in depth made it difficult for the submarine to track the targets it had detected since the previous day, and which were now so close. Membrana and his crew had bought, albeit inadvertently, more precious time for the Argentine Task Force.

By comparing information from either side, it is now possible to determine that *Splendid* was on the point of being detected by the Tracker. However, with its silent design, and the fact that the Tracker was not capable of monitoring all its sonobuoys at the same time, this detection was not made.

The erstwhile uneventful nocturnal flight, however, would present some other challenges to the crew of 2-AS-22 when it came to try to get the aircraft back on deck once its mission was over. It just so happened that fog had reduced visibility on the flight deck.

The commander finally managed to get the aircraft back on board around 0625 hrs, after its second approach (and after the Landing Ship Officer or LSO had had the lights of the ship turned on, so the aircraft was better able to orientate itself) following one of the longest flights by a Tracker during the conflict. As then *Teniente* Membrana later recalled:

> We flew on the night of 3 May (leaving around 2350 hrs) along with 'Negro' Ottogalli to cover the crossing of the mouth of Golfo San Jorge. Everything went well until we were delayed in our return to the ship. On reaching "Bingo 3" (in other words, we were very low on fuel) we requested to be guided to the carrier. But, close to it, we had a cold sweat as it turned out there was a dense fog between us and the flight deck.
>
> The first approach was aborted following advice from *Santísima Trinidad*, because the radar on the aircraft carrier was guiding us towards the stern of the oiler *Punta Médanos*, which was located close by *25 de Mayo*.
>
> On the second approach we got to around half a mile and we still couldn't see anything. At that moment, Covarrubias, who was the LSO, told us in a calm voice: 'Don't descend any further', and for a second, he switched on the lights which indicated the direction that we needed to fly. However, at that moment we saw them above us (not below us as they should have been). A quick glance at the altimeter showed that we were at just 75 feet! The water was not at all far below us. We lined up and hooked onto the arrestor wire and felt the relief as we felt that a thousand hands were pulling us hard back onto the deck. When we finally stopped at the end of the sudden deceleration, one of the engines failed as they had run out of fuel. But the mission was already history, and with a slight tremble in my hands I switched everything off.

The daytime approach was done either visually or by instruments while the night-time approach was always made using instruments only. The visual approach was always much easier to fly, starting with first flying a down-wind leg of a landing circuit, then making a turn that lined the aircraft up on finals and under the control of the LSO who gave fluidity and security to the manoeuvre. Of course, there were far more complications during night-time operations. During this, the radar control vectored the aircraft when at six miles from the stern of the ship, thus putting it on finals. A missed approach was only carried out if the carrier was not in view at half a mile and at an altitude of one hundred feet, in other words when almost on deck.

The stern of an aircraft carrier is not a friendly place: the LSO is situated a few feet from tonnes of metal descending towards the ship and open to the elements and weather (however, they are permitted certain freedoms about their uniforms – an example being an officer that used a bearskin cap). During the recovery of aircraft, the LSO was the boss of the ship and what happened on the flight deck. He could suggest to the ship's commander, for example, a change in course or speed, all with the safety of the returning aircraft in mind.

The destroyer ARA *Hércules* during fleet exercises. First in the line is the cruiser ARA *General Belgrano*, starting a turn to starboard. (Via Francisco Kawa)

ELMA *Formosa.* (HMS *Splendid* Report of Proceedings)

The Argentine fleet changed course at 0735 hrs to a west north-west heading to enter Golfo San Jorge and proceeded to sail around the edge of it. The destroyers had experienced greater fuel consumption than had been anticipated and had broken off to carry out a refuelling. The *Py* had just re-joined the Task Force. That same afternoon the two Type 42 destroyers would also abandon *25 de Mayo* for a few hours to carry out a furtive refuelling with the fleet oiler close to the Isla Escondida.

Exactly two hours after beginning to navigate around the gulf, 2-AS-24 was launched under the command of *Capitán de Corbeta* Héctor "*Yunque*" ("Anvil") Skare, the unit commander, with the crew of *Teniente de Fragata* Sanguinetti and NCOs R. Lencina and I. Lencina. "*Yunque*" was an old timer when it came to embarked air operations. He had carried out the fourth Argentine landing on deck on *25 de Mayo* and years later had been its Operations Officer.

The sortie did not have any incidents of note except that, as with all the other Tracker sorties, there was a terrible cold inside the aircraft which chilled its occupants to the bone. The cabin heater was in the nose of the aircraft and worked by burning aviation fuel. It was not popular amongst the crew as it tended to fail (and could also catch fire at the same time) while at the same time its use also reduced the endurance of the aircraft. 2-AS-24 landed back on deck at 1340 hrs, having only managed to detect a few cargo and fishing vessels.

HMS *Splendid*, however, had not been in the location that *Capitán* Skare had been searching. Around 0647 hrs it had regained contact with one large contact and three small ones and was moving into position to be able to carry out an attack with Mk 8 torpedoes, which had already been loaded into the tubes. These contacts were ARA *25 de Mayo* and its escorts. In the area there were also other ships, which the commander of the submarine estimated to be the corvettes and were second priority targets. However, the submarine was unable to fire its torpedoes that morning. It had lost contact with some of the targets and others were now inside the Twelve-Mile Limit of the Argentine territorial waters which prevented them from being engaged according to the Rules of Engagement. Everything just seemed to happen too quickly. The juicy enemy ships had managed to evade attack.

At 0924 hrs, filled with anxiety, Commander Lane-Nott raised the periscope, prepared to identify and sink contact "S-52". This was the only one that hadn't been able to escape the clutches of the submarine.

ARA *Alferez Sobral*. This converted tug (ex-USS *Salish*) was attacked on 3 May by Sea Skua missiles launched by Sea Lynx helicopters from both HMS *Glasgow* and *Coventry*. In spite of sustaining serious damage it remained afloat. Her commander, *Capitán de Corbeta* Sergio Gómez Roca, died on the bridge during the attack. (via Enrique Fortini)

This had previously been classified when first detected as a warship, with an estimated speed of 11 knots and at 5,000 yards. The sailors ran to their combat positions, the moment they had spent their careers training for had finally arrived. The moment of truth that would possibly change naval history.

However, it was an enormous disappointment for the crew of *Splendid* when the contact was finally identified from 2,750 yards, as being the Argentine cargo ship ELMA *Formosa*. The ship was completing its return from the Falklands/Malvinas and had been attacked during its long journey, by aircraft from the Argentine Air Force, which had resulted in an unexploded bomb being lodged in its hold. A detailed sketch in *Splendid's* logbook proves that the *Formosa* was, effectively, the target that was stalked that day, but not sunk.

It is possible that Lane-Nott had not wanted to reveal his presence in the area by attacking a merchant ship. He had surely estimated that attacking a support ship that was returning to port empty simply did not justify risking the hunt that they would be subjected to afterwards. As it was, ELMA *Formosa* had also helped the Task Force as it had distracted the British submarine for a few precious minutes.

Later, *Splendid* would also stalk a large tanker that it could not identify, much to the chagrin of the commander, who would later call it a "day of frustrations". It had been a really disheartening day. The previous day they had located the Argentine Task Force in open sea, and on 4 May he cornered it and had almost got into a firing position.

However, *Splendid* had not managed to take the next step and had not risked itself in combat. Obviously, it was in a different situation to the one that *Conqueror* had found itself in. They were in shallow waters and the anti-submarine effort had been multiplied by aerial assets.

Returning to the Argentine air operations, at 1455 hrs Tracker 2-AS-22 took off again in an anti-submarine configuration. This time it was being flown under the command of the squadron XO, *Capitán de Corbeta* Covarrubias (with the remaining crew made up of *Teniente de Fragata* Marinsalta and NCOs Vallejos and Cufre). The aircraft detected and identified the *Formosa* and another three vessels with the ESM equipment, which it classified as civilian traffic. They landed back on deck at 1935 hrs. The radar of *Capitán* Covarrubias' Tracker was also detected and classified by *Splendid* at 1804 hrs, adding to the tension on board the submarine.

Other than these three anti-submarine sorties flown that day, the squadron also flew some surface search sorties to locate the patrol vessel ARA *Alférez Sobral*, which had been attacked two days previously when it had entered the Total Exclusion Zone while attempting to rescue the crew of an Air Force Canberra bomber that had been shot down.

These sorties were flown by Tracker 2-AS-26 under the command of *Capitán de Corbeta* Dabini (with the crew made up of *Teniente de Corbeta* Bazán and NCOs Paulinkas and Condorí), which was launched at 1616 hrs and landed on deck at 1720 hrs; and by Tracker 2-AS-22 under the command of *Capitán de Corbeta* "Checho" Goitía (along with *Teniente de Corbeta* Núñez, and NCOs Conde and Carrera), which was launched at 2340 hrs and landed on deck at 0118 hrs the following day. Tracker 2-AS-26 also flew a later troublesome nocturnal sortie which had to divert to Trelew due to a problem with one of its engines. It returned to the ship at 0903 hrs the next day.

It is also worth mentioning that on this same day the Argentine Naval Air Arm had managed to deliver a tremendous blow to the British by putting HMS *Sheffield* out of action, following an attack

HMS *Sheffield* ablaze after being hit on 4 May 1982. (MoD)

by the Exocet armed Super Etendards of the Second Fighter and Attack Naval Air Squadron (*Segunda Escuadrilla Aeronaval de Caza y Ataque*).

There was a certain degree of euphoria on board *25 de Mayo* on the night of the 4th May, the product of the news of the successful attack on the British destroyer. Those on-board felt that this compensated somewhat for the loss of the *General Belgrano*, whose survivors were just beginning to be rescued. The Operations Officer on-board *25 de Mayo* recalled the feelings experienced on the ship's bridge:

> The sinking of the *Belgrano* pulled a cloak of bitterness and worry over the ship. The commanders of each ship were friends and comrades. The Engineering Officer on the *Belgrano* was a colleague and friend of mine. The hours following the sinking, until we heard of the rescue of survivors and their names started to appear on lists, were spent in a state of great anxiety on the bridge of the aircraft carrier, where we were practically living. The successful attack on the *Sheffield* produced a level of joy that lifted some of the tension and worry that we were suffering from.

"The enemy isn't invincible" was the obligatory comment oft repeated by many during that time.

7

5 MAY – PROBSUB!

> "Take her up to periscope depth," he ordered. "It's time to check for orders, and we'll try an ESM sweep to see what's happening." Not a simple procedure, that. The submarine came up slowly, cautiously, turning to allow her sonar to make certain that there was not a ship around. "Raise the ESM." An electronics technician pressed the button to raise the mast for his broad-band receiver. The board lit up instantly. "Numerous electronic sources, sir. Three J-band search sets, lots of other stuff. Lots of VHF and UHF chatter. The recorders are going." *That figures,* McCafferty thought. *The odds against having anyone here after us are pretty low, though.* "Up scope." The captain angled the search-scope lens upward to scan the sky for a nearby aircraft and made a quick turn around the horizon. He noticed something odd, and had to angle down the lens to see what it was. There was a green smoke marker not two hundred yards away. McCafferty cringed and spun the instrument back around. A multi-engine aircraft was coming out of the haze—directly in at them. The captain reached up and spun the periscope wheel, lowering the instrument. *"Take her down!* All ahead flank! Make your depth eight hundred feet!" *Where the hell did he come from?* The submarine's engines fairly exploded into action. A flurry of orders had the helmsmen push their controls to the stops. *"Torpedo in the water, starboard side!"* a sonarnan screamed. (Red Storm Rising, Tom Clancy)

HMS *Conqueror* (Artwork by Javier "Javo" Ruberto)

HMS *Onyx* (Artwork by Javier "Javo" Ruberto)

HMS *Splendid* (Artwork by Javier "Javo" Ruberto)

S61D4 Sea King 2-H-231, Second Helicopter Naval Air Squadron (*Segunda Escuadrilla Aeronaval de Helicópteros*), aircraft carrier ARA *25 de Mayo*, May 1982. (Artwork by Javier "Javo" Ruberto)

S-2E Tracker 2-AS-24, Anti-Submarine Naval Air Squadron (*Escuadrilla Aeronaval Antisubmarina*), aircraft carrier ARA *25 de Mayo*, May 1982. (Artwork Javier "Javo" Ruberto)

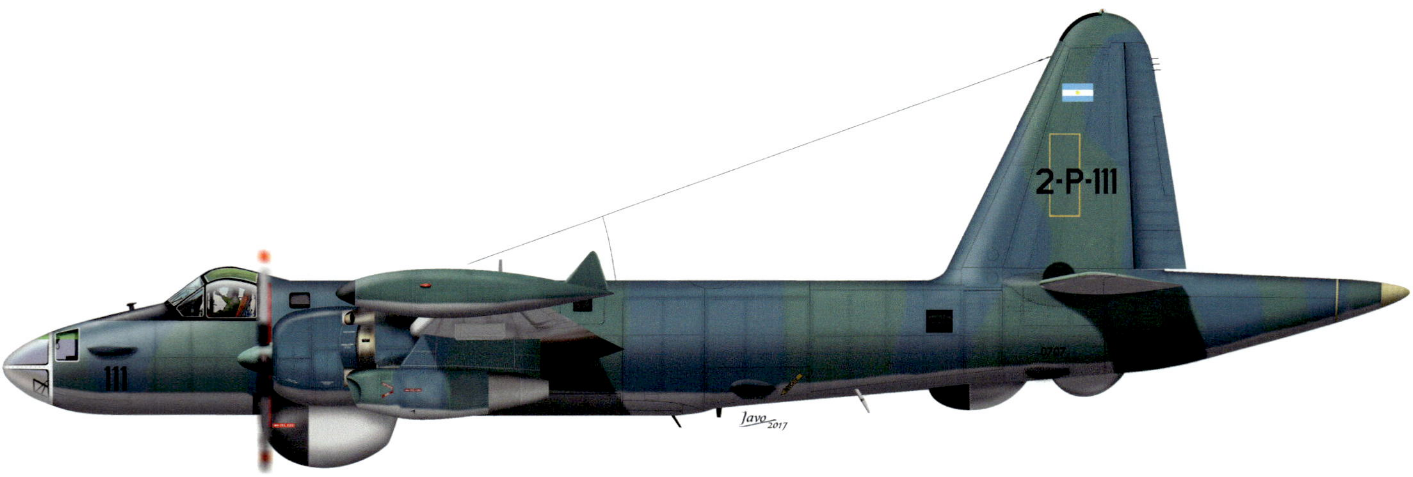

SP-2H Neptune 2-P-111, Reconnaissance Naval Air Squadron (*Escuadrilla Aeronaval de Exploración*), Base Aeronaval Almirante Hermes Quijada, Río Grande, Tierra del Fuego, May 1982. (Artwork by Javier "Javo" Ruberto)

Fokker F27-400M Troopship TC-78, First Air Brigade, I Air Transport Group, IV Air Transport Sqn (*I Brigada Aérea, Grupo I de Transporte Aéreo, Escuadrón IV de Transporte Aéreo,*) Base Aérea Militar Comodoro Rivadavia, Comodoro Rivadavia, Chubut, May 1982. (Artwork by Javier "Javo" Ruberto)

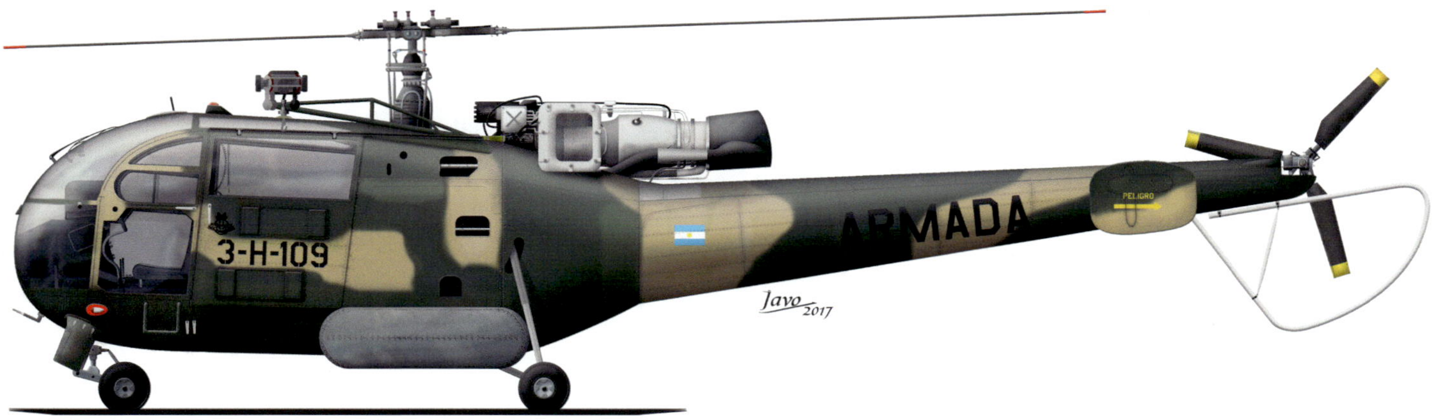

SA 319 Alouette III 3-H-109, First Helicopter Naval Air Squadron (*Primera Escuadrilla Aeronaval de Helicópteros*), aircraft carrier ARA *25 de Mayo*, May 1982. (Artwork by Javier "Javo" Ruberto)

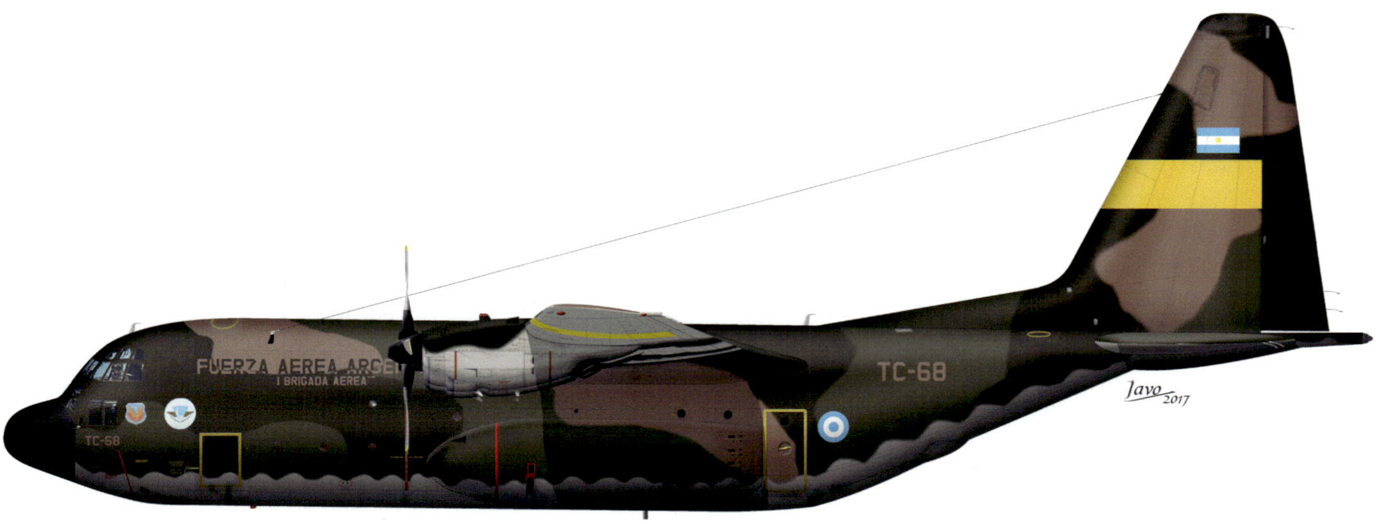

C-130H Hercules TC-68, First Air Brigade, I Air Transport Group, I Air Transport Sqn (*I Brigada Aérea, Grupo I de Transporte Aéreo, Escuadrón I de Transporte Aéreo*), Base Aérea Militar Comodoro Rivadavia, Comodoro Rivadavia, Chubut, May 1982. (Artwork by Javier "Javo" Ruberto)

Boeing 707-372C TC-92, First Air Brigade, I Air Transport Group, V Air Transport Sqn (*I Brigada Aérea, Grupo I de Transporte Aéreo, Escuadrón V de Transporte Aéreo*), Base Aérea Militar El Palomar, Buenos Aires, May 1982. (Artwork by Javier "Javo" Ruberto)

Tu-95RTs (Bear D), 392nd Independent Long-Range Reconnaissance Aviation Regiment (*392nd Otdyel'nyy Dal'nye Razvedyvatel'nyy Aviatsionnyy Polk*), Luanda (Angola), May 1982. (Artwork by Javier "Javo" Ruberto)

A-4Q Skyhawk 3-A-314, Third Fighter and Attack Naval Squadron (*Tercera Escuadrilla Aeronaval de Caza y Ataque*), aircraft carrier ARA *25 de Mayo*, May 1982. (Artwork by Javier "Javo" Ruberto)

ARA *25 de Mayo* in the South Atlantic, before the 1982 conflict. A Sea King, two Alouette helicopters, and five A-4Q Skyhawk are on the flight deck. (*Armada Argentina*)

Another view of the ARA *25 de Mayo* before the war, showing her with the catapult on steam and turning into the wind to launch four A-4Q Skyhawks on a training sortie. (*Armada Argentina*)

View from the bridge towards the stern of the ARA *25 de Mayo*, showing all the carrier-available types as of 1 May 1982, including seven A-4Q Skyhawks of the *Tercera Escuadrilla Aeronaval de Caza y Ataque* (foreground), and four S-2E Trackers of the *Escuadrilla Aeronaval Antisubmarina.* (Via Juan José Membrana)

Tracker 2-AS-22 at Stanley Airport (*Base Aérea Militar Malvinas*). Two Tracker aircraft operated from the island´s airport, between 3 and 13 April 1982. (Via Juan José Membrana)

Argentine Air Force Fokker F-27 Troopship TC-78. (Alejandro Amendolara)

Dense fog, as seen in this pre-war photograph, repeatedly reduced the visibility around the ARA *25 de Mayo* during the nights from 1 to 2 May, 2 to 3 May, and 3 to 4 May 1982, making flight operations extremely dangerous. (Via Tom Cooper)

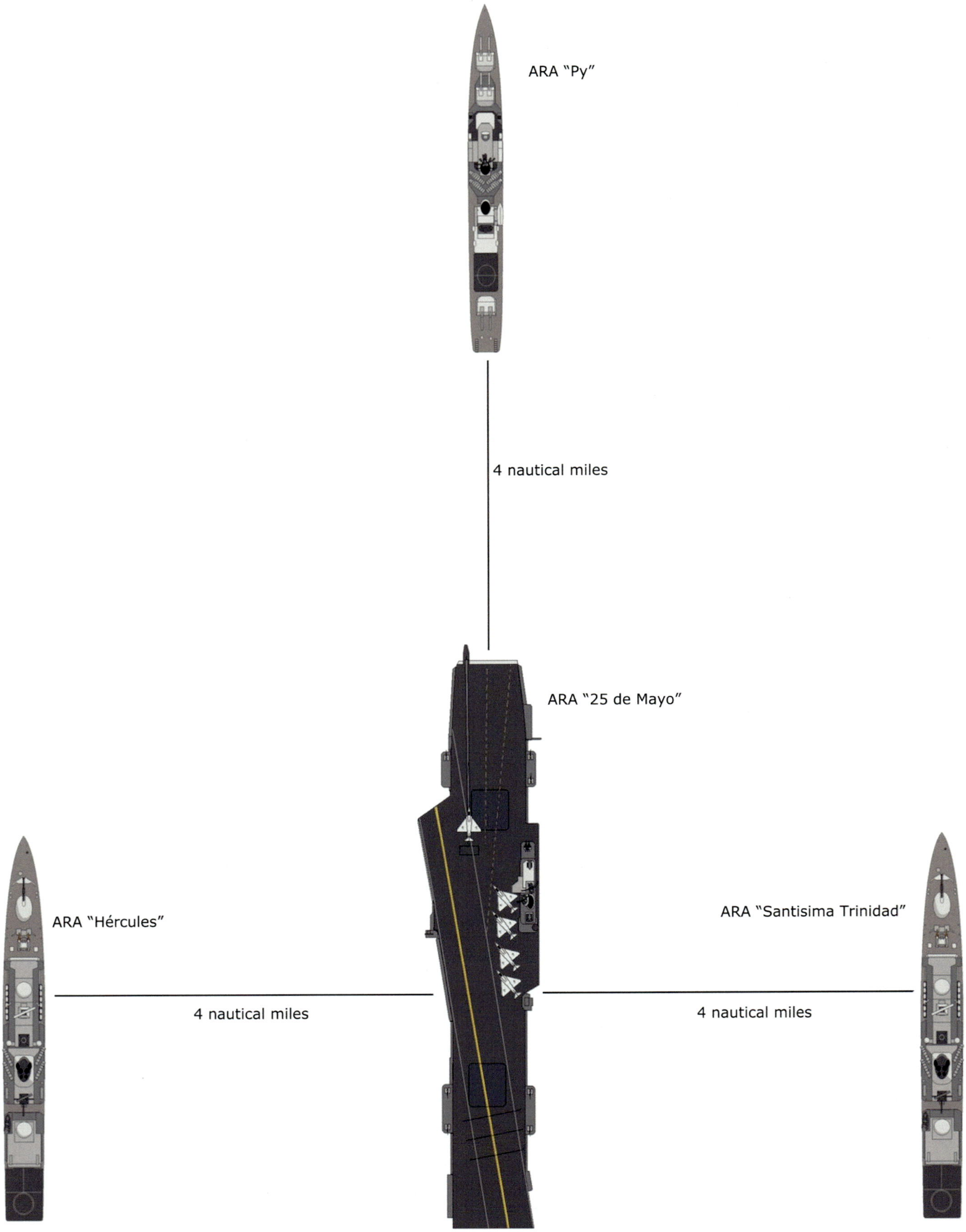

Defensive screen of the ARA *25 de Mayo*. (Artwork by Planeman)

An S-2E Tracker folding its wings on the deck, shortly after landing during an exercise in November 1981. (via Enrique Fortini)

Probably the same aircraft (2-AS-26), seen while being lowered down the bow elevator, minutes after landing. Visible in the rear are a Sea King helicopter, and the fin of a Skyhawk. (via Enrique Fortini)

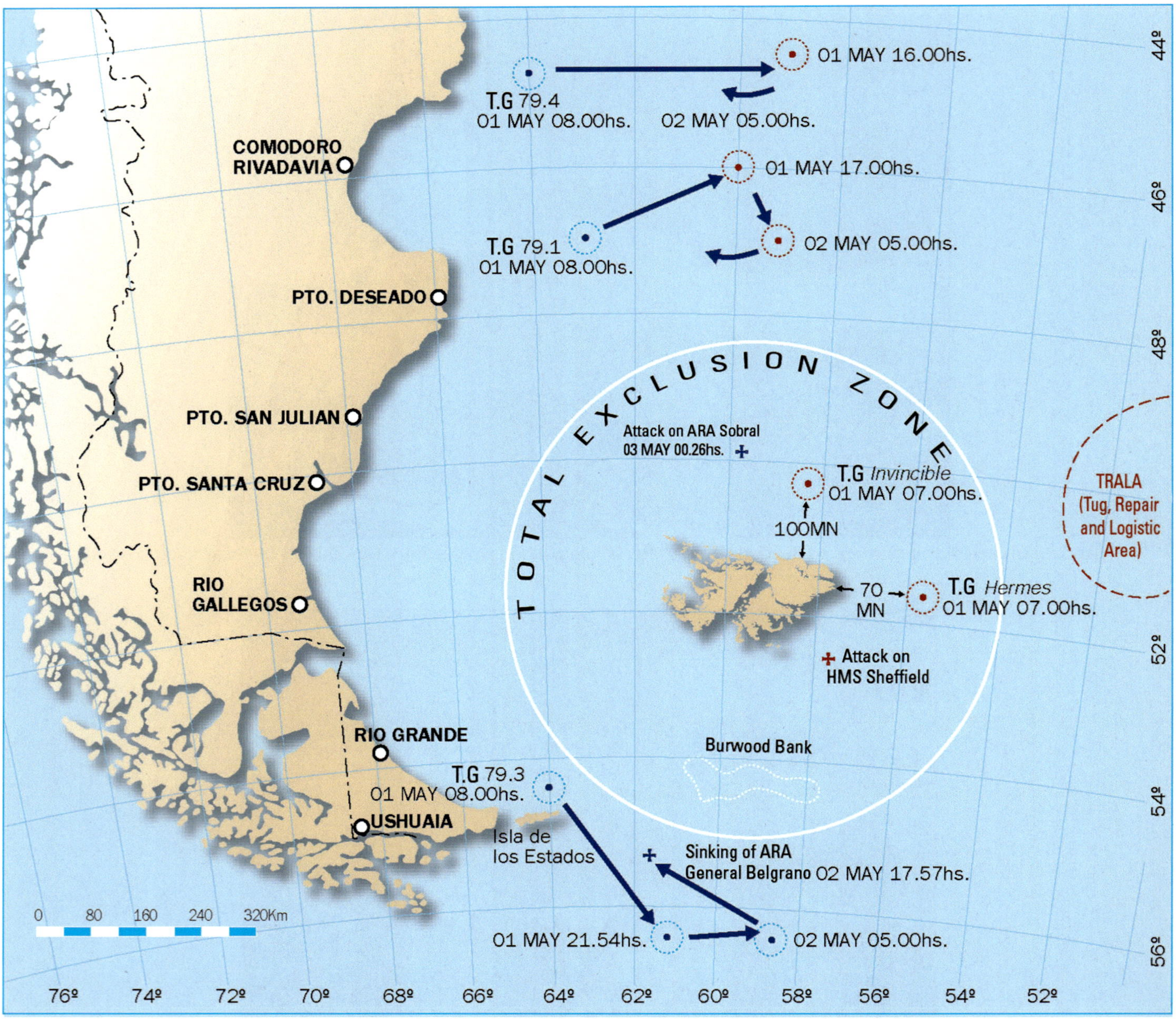

Argentine Naval Operations from 1 to 4 May

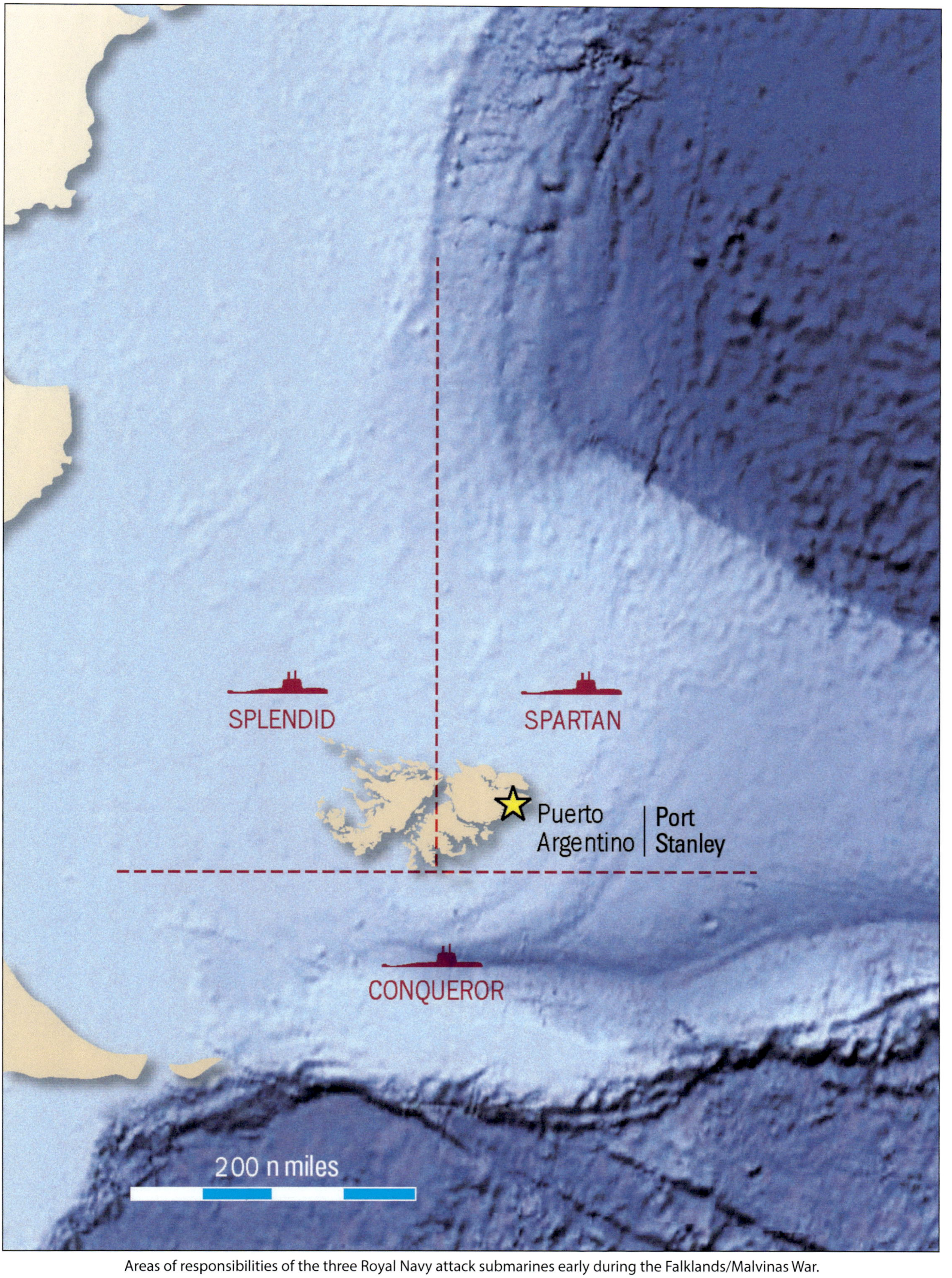

Areas of responsibilities of the three Royal Navy attack submarines early during the Falklands/Malvinas War.

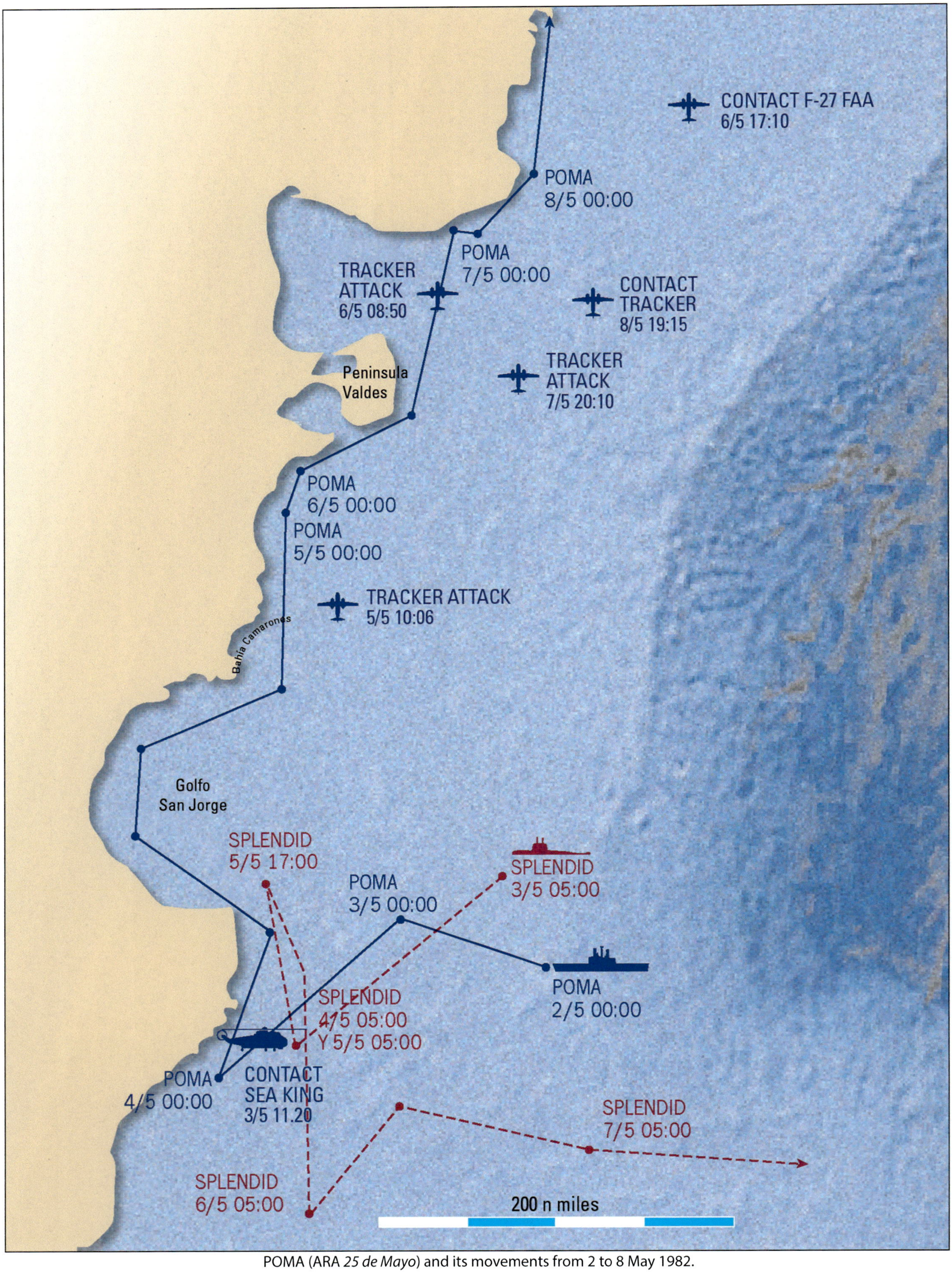

POMA (ARA *25 de Mayo*) and its movements from 2 to 8 May 1982.

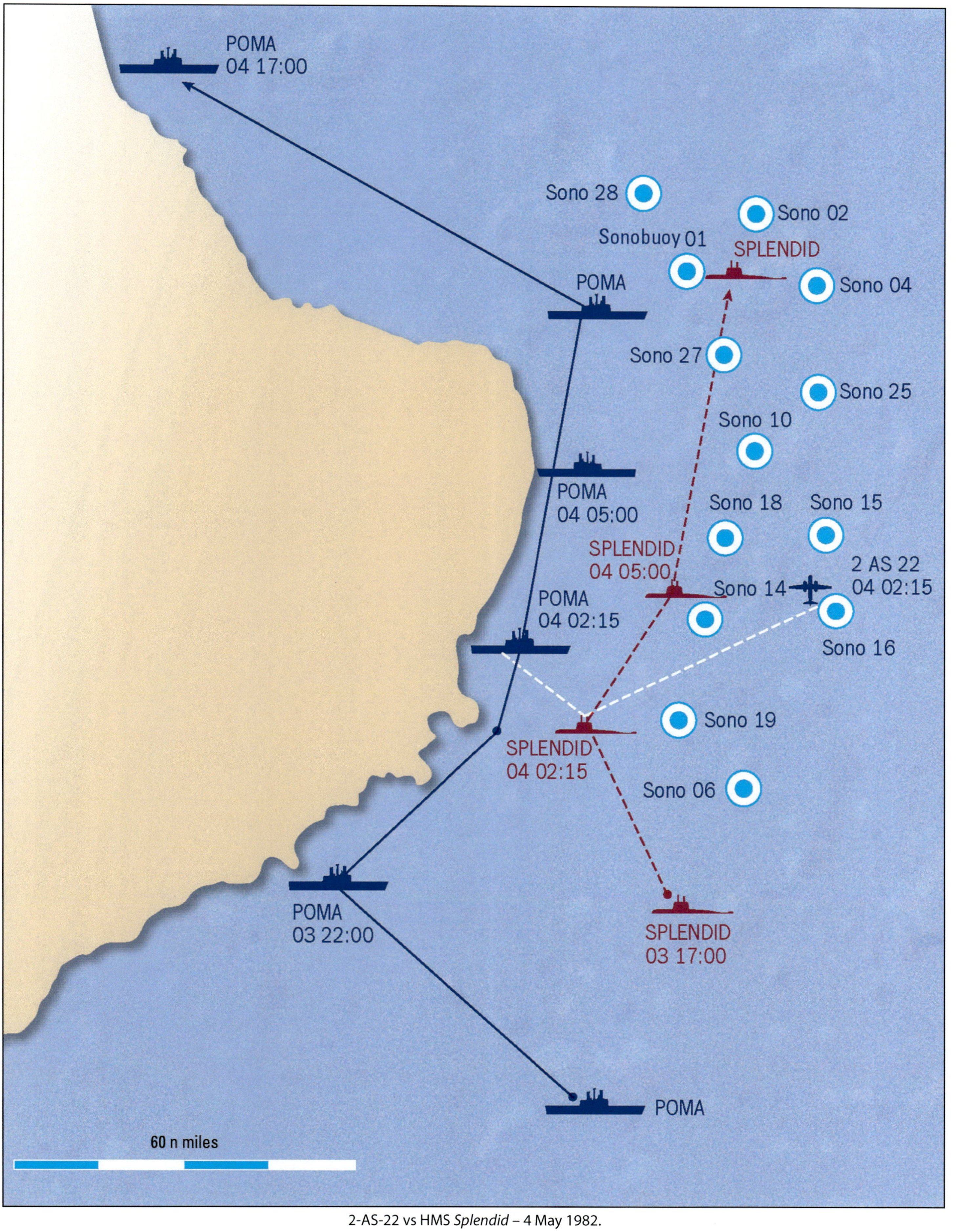

2-AS-22 vs HMS *Splendid* – 4 May 1982.

5 May, attack on a submerged intruder.

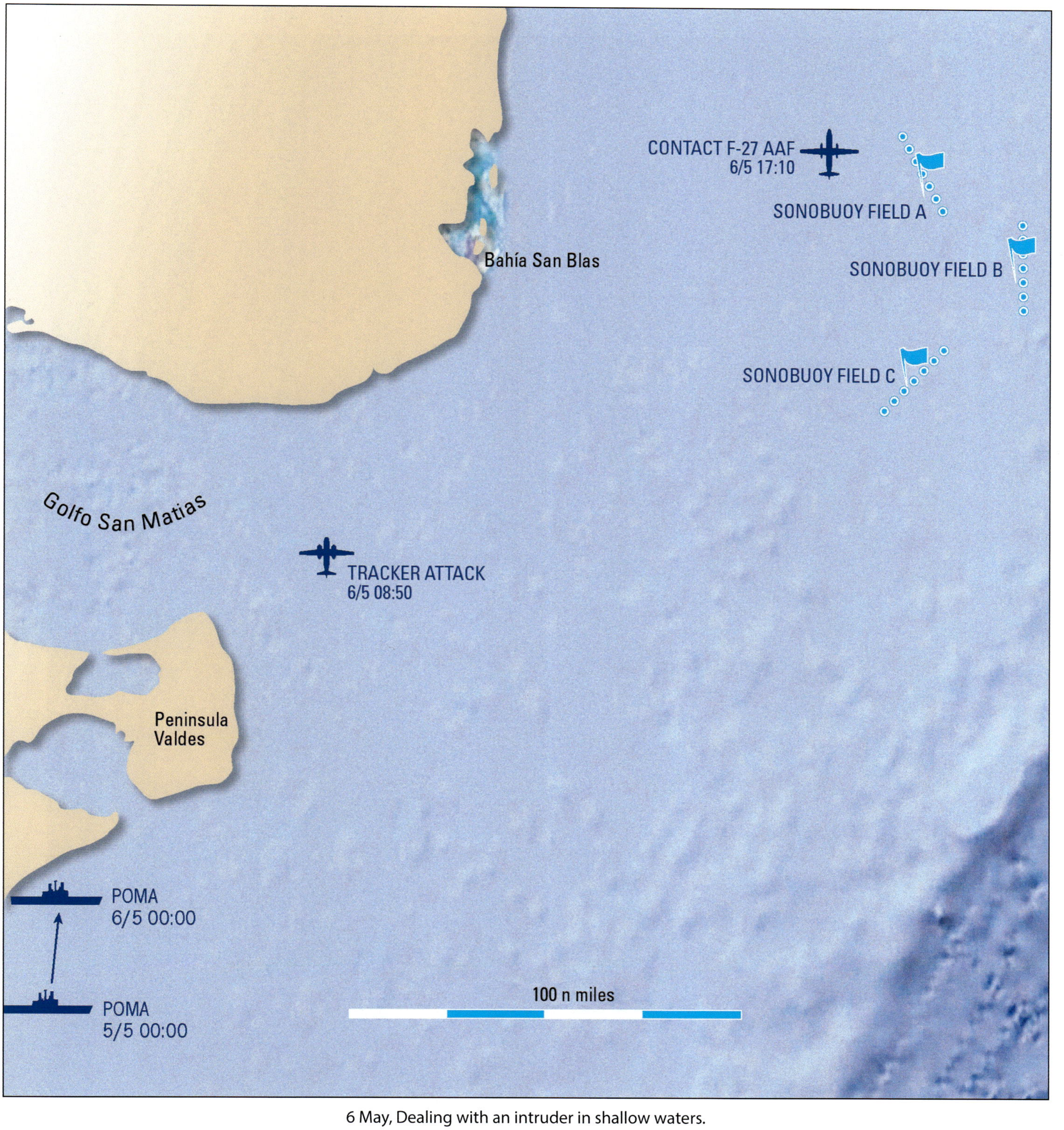

6 May, Dealing with an intruder in shallow waters.

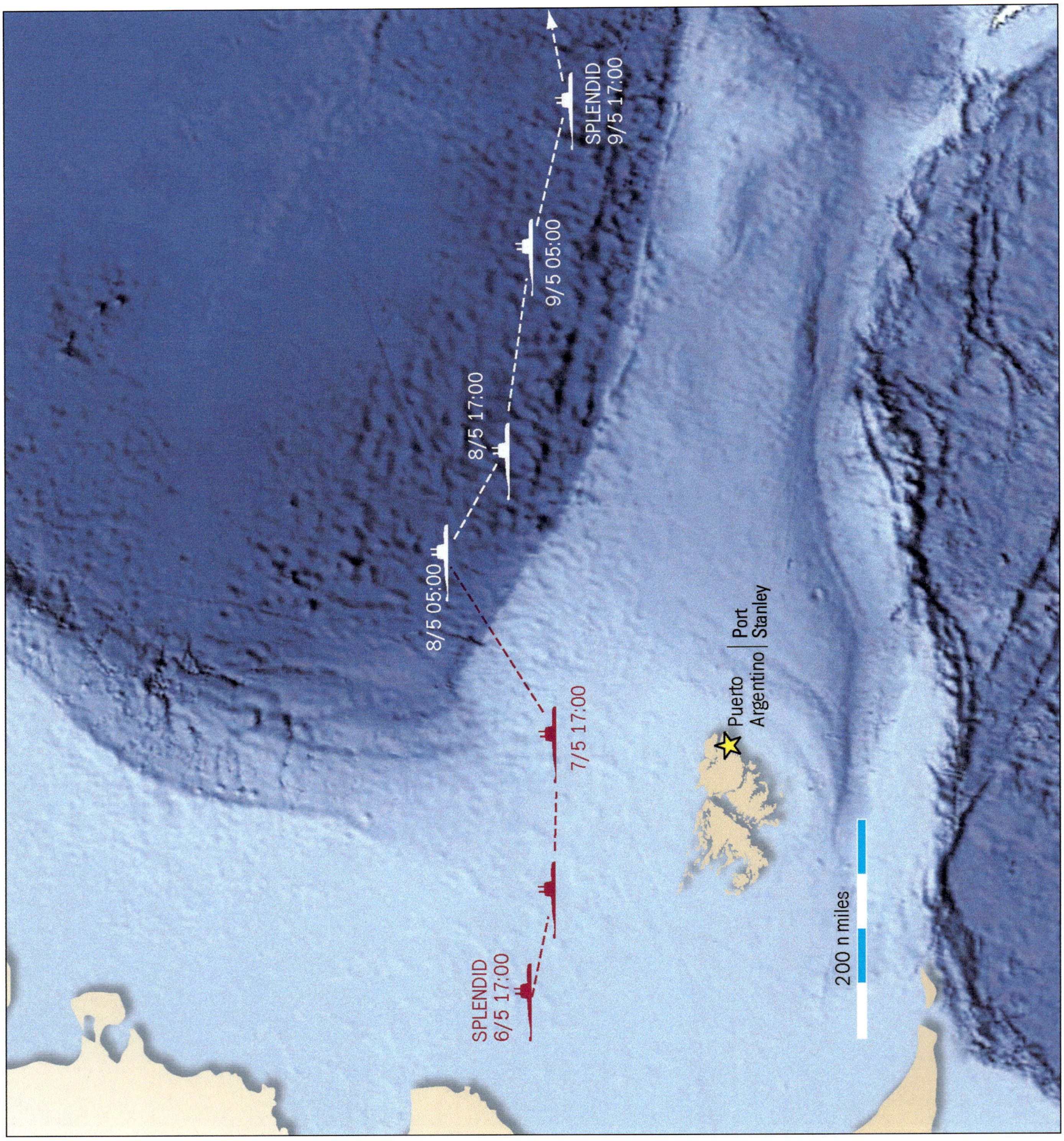

HMS *Splendid* moving east to undertake repairs.

A Mk. 46 torpedo in flight. The Royal Navy dropped a total of 26 Mk. 46 torpedoes, seven Mk. 44 torpedoes and 47 Mk. 11 Depth Charges during Operation *Corporate*. (US Navy)

During the first hours of the 5th May some requests for help were received on a frequency of 500 Khz and it was assumed that they were coming from ARA *Sobral*. Another Tracker sortie was prepared with the aim of investigating the source of these distress calls. The squadron rushed to get 2-AS-23 ready and the crew were chosen. This sortie was to be led by *Teniente de Navío* Carlos Cal, an experienced anti-submarine commander. When the conflict broke, he was serving as a flight instructor at the Naval Aviation School at Punta Indio. Following the success of Operation *Rosario* and the consequences of the British preparing a task force, there was a sudden requirement for reinforcement pilots and signallers for the operational squadrons. Cal was quickly posted back to the squadron, but first carried out flight tests on Tracker 2-AS-23, following the completion of its hurriedly finished major inspection.

2-AS-23 was embarked on the carrier as a spare. As it had been pushed rapidly through its inspection, it had yet to have its electronic detection equipment reinstalled and so only had its surface search radar on board. As the sortie was only one of search and rescue, this aircraft was selected as it lacked its MAD, sonobuoy equipment and ESM equipment. This equipment was not necessary for such a task.

Guardiamarina Gustavo "Gachi" Ferrari was designated as co-pilot, who had been with the squadron for scarcely three months having only gained his pilot's wings in 1981. This was a perfect opportunity for his baptism of fire and build up flight hours. However, he hadn't yet fully completed his training as an operational Tracker co-pilot due to the lack of time. The sensor operators were the experienced *Suboficial Segundo* Rodolfo Lencina and *Cabo Segundo* Enzo Panaritti, who was also on his first tour with the unit.

Regardless of 2-AS-23's operative deficiencies, the aircraft was armed with one Mk 44 homing torpedo along with some sonobuoys and smoke markers. This was the standard weapons load for the Tracker, regardless of the assigned mission.

The Tracker was launched from *25 de Mayo* at 0705 hrs whilst it was sailing at a point level with Bahía de los Huesos, located in Chubut province. A smooth climb to 3,000 feet followed in the clarity of the first light of the day, in a calm air and in the cold of the morning. This allowed the crew to relax a bit following the tension of the launch from the carrier.

After around a half hour of flight, as was routine, a radar search was carried out. This was usually accomplished by lowering the radome and transmitting solely towards the rear of the aircraft in order not to alert any possible enemy in the bow. The operator calibrated the antenna using the echoes from the carrier and its escorts that were some 60 miles to the rear.

The visibility was perfect, with an almost perfectly calm wind, flat sea and the dawn light making everything towards the east visible, where the sun was soon to rise.

Before the test was completed the pilot ordered a couple of turns towards the horizon, to verify the situation on the surface in front of the aircraft. At this same moment, at 0743 hrs, *Teniente* Cal spotted in the distance a line in the sea, the type of line that would be left if a submarine was sailing at periscope depth with its masts above the surface and leaving their typical wake. Seconds later the radar operator announced on the intercom: *"I have a goblin. Bearing zero nine zero – 10 miles"*.

Having then arrived three minutes later over this datum, the whole crew observed an object that appeared to be a submarine's snorkel (being crowned with a small exhaust trail) disappearing from the surface and heading towards the north, while at the same time vanishing from the radar screen.

As the commander of the Task Force had already instructed that any submarine contact must be attacked, *Teniente* Cal ordered the launch of the Mk 44 torpedo and a passive sonobuoy on top of the intruder, located at latitude 44° 40' S, longitude 64° 40'W.

Following the torpedo drop, no explosion was observed. Nor were the crew able to follow the torpedo run, as the aircraft still lacked the equipment to be able to listen to the sonobuoy.

The torpedo, as with all of those used during the duration of the conflict, had been pre-calibrated to search up to 120 feet depth and without a minimum attack depth. As there was no other way of launching another attack (no other weapons were onboard), the Tracker, after orbiting the area for a while then returned to its original surface search mission.

At 0805 hrs, after having received the report from *Teniente* Cal of the attack on a submarine, the alert helicopter on the carrier, Sea King 2-H-231 manned (again) by *Teniente de Navío* Osvaldo Iglesias and *Teniente de Navío* Guillermo Iglesias, was launched. The two Iglesias now had another opportunity to confront the enemy in the depths. The crew was composed by *Teniente de Fragata* García, *Suboficial Segundo* Ponce and *Cabo Principal* Ramos.

At 0847 hrs, the second Sea King took off from the carrier. It was 2-H-234 commanded by *Capitán de Corbeta* Norberto "Rufo" Barro, the squadron commander (along with *Teniente de Fragata* Urbano, *Suboficial Segundo* Soruco, *Suboficial Primero* S. Alvarez and *Suboficial Segundo* Llanos). The helicopters, which represented all the Sea Kings available for operations in the Argentine Navy, each carried a load of two Mk 44 anti-submarine torpedoes.

At the same time, the activity within the Tracker squadron was also frenetic. As *Teniente* "Quique" Fortini remembered:

> It was early, I think I was still in my cabin, already awake and up since a flight had just been launched and my cabinmate, *Teniente* Osvaldo Iglesias, had just left to be on duty in the alert Sea King.
>
> At that moment, *Capitán* Skare called me and told me to come to the Pilot's Ready Room. He also told me that Charlie Cal had detected a small contact and that I was going on the next sortie, which would leave after the Sea Kings. This was more than enough for me to know that a good day's hunting was awaiting us, and together with my crew, we started the pre-flight briefing.

Finally, a minute after Barro's Sea King took off, the Tracker commanded by Fortini, 2-AS-24, was launched from the carrier. *Teniente de Navío* Carlos "Chingolo" Ferrer and *Suboficial*es Raimondo and Cufre were also crewmembers. Fortini was fully aware of the task entrusted to him, being completely sure that his friend and colleague Cal could not have been mistaken. "We're going to hunt a real submarine" he was thinking to himself as the sortie started.

Sea King 2-H-231 was the first to arrive at the datum. It immediately started its anti-submarine search. Hover, lower the sonar and listen. Nothing. Sonar up, change position and repeat. Always with passive sonar.

The second Sea King was unable to do the same. It suffered problems that meant it was unable to start to use its detection equipment. All the same, *Capitán* Barro decided to stay in the area in support of the search with all the eyes of the anxious crew scrutinising the surface of the sea. After a couple of dips of the sonar, the Observer on-board 2-H-231, *Teniente de Fragata* Edgardo García (an officer with solid experience in the operation of the dipping sonar), gained a faint hydroponic contact on his sonar and updated the datum to latitude 44º27'S, longitude 64º19'W.

Unfortunately, when he turned on the recorder that was incorporated in the sonar equipment (which would permit the later analysis of the contact), it short-circuited and began to emit sparks. *Teniente* García immediately turned it off. He already had too many things going on to add a fire in his console too. The contact was not strong. The audio of the contact emitted a light buzz like a lightweight propeller but made it very difficult for the operator to calculate the revolutions it was producing. With such a lack of data, the target could not be positively identified by the Observer. However, after having analysed the signal arriving at the sonar for some time, it was estimated that the contact was moving away from the helicopter at a speed of around four to six knots. In his opinion this was a POSSUB Confidence 2/4, and he proceeded to classify it as such.

In the Argentine Navy, contacts that could possibly be a submarine were classified according to the following levels of certainty:

1. Confirmed Submarine. (CERTSUB) A contact has been sighted and positively identified by competent personnel as a submarine.
2. Probable Submarine. (PROBSUB) A contact displaying strong cumulative evidence of being a submarine. This classification is normally based on the information gathered by either sonar or radar. The officer in charge gives a confidence level, from 1 (the lowest) to 4 (the highest)
3. Possible Submarine. (POSSUB) A contact on which available information indicates the likely presence of a submarine, however there is insufficient evidence to justify a higher classification. The level of confidence is also graded from 1 to 4.
4. No Submarine. (NONSUB) A contact has characteristics that exclude the possibility that it is a submarine.

The contact was maintained for nearly an hour, on coherent acoustic frequencies and bearings. It certainly wasn't a biological contact (for example, a whale or shoal of fish) nor a false signal. It was something mechanical and submerged.

Obviously, this new detection had not gone unnoticed in *Teniente* Fortini's Tracker which had just arrived on the scene. Taking up the search, they deployed three passive sonobuoys in an Alpha trajectory (a triangle deployment with its centre on a fixed point established by the helicopter) to cover any possible escape route for the submarine.

The commander of the Tracker decided to initiate, according to doctrine, a search with the MAD equipment. This involved flying at extremely low level, with the MAD boom, the detection equipment for detecting magnetic anomalies, extended from the rear of the aircraft. Each time the reading on the equipment went over a certain value, in other words each time they flew over something ferrous, they would drop a smoke marker on the spot. They made a turn and carried out the first pass of their search: the needle on the MAD instrument on the pilot's console jumped. They dropped a smoke marker on the spot. However, the operator located in the centre of the aircraft shouted, *"No MAD"* over the intercom. He made this call as, according to his training, the values analysed did not correspond to a submerged ferrous object. They carried out a second pass and, once again, there was a movement on the needle on the instrument. Once again, a smoke marker was dropped. Again, a second later the operator, this time with a calmer voice, indicated that the contact did not correspond to a submarine.

At first, *Teniente* Fortini thought that they had passed over an old shipwreck. However, he was then surprised to see that the second smoke marker was some hundreds of feet from the first. Although, in line with the operator's training the contact was not a submarine, it was most certainly something that was moving. The third pass only strengthened this theory. They continued with the search for the next fifteen minutes, making a further nine passes and gaining eight contacts. The smoke markers from this effort drew a line towards the open sea.

Meanwhile, at around 1006 hrs, Sea King 2-H-231 was still following the contact on its sonar and had noticed the contact had increased its speed and the plot was coherent with a submarine. *Teniente de Navío* Iglesias then decided to try out one of the novel tactics developed by the squadron, as noted previously, for carrying out a passive search and attack. The helicopter began repositioning at various points along the bearing and dipping the sonar, with the aim of finally finding themselves directly above the contact.

Sonar up, climb, transit to a new position, hover and descend and dip – a roller-coaster ride with the Sea King's turbines roaring at full power. After a couple of jumps, *Teniente* Garcia turned the dial on the console and determined that the bearing of the submarine had inverted, which meant that the helicopter had overtaken the supposed submarine. With that, the crew finally convinced themselves that the contact they were chasing was an intelligent submerged vehicle. Therefore, the Observer raised the classification to PROBSUB Confidence 1.

The moment to make a deliberate attack had arrived. Nobody was surprised, therefore, when *Teniente* Fortini announced, in his capacity as Scene of Action Commander (SAC), that he had decided to drop a torpedo. Everybody there were convinced that they were hunting a British submarine. As they were the last unit to update the position of the contact, Sea King 2-H-231 guided the Tracker to the correct position to drop its weapon (a VECTAC).

Teniente Fortini threw the aircraft into an abrupt turn, accelerated, and fixed his sight on the surface of the sea, where there was absolutely nothing. Underneath that spot lurked a submarine to defeat. To his right, his co-pilot confirmed that the arming sequence on the weapons panel had been completed. Tracker 2-AS-24 began its run to the weapon drop point. The crew on-board felt a new vibration as the doors of the weapons bay opened. And, moments later, the twin-engine aircraft leapt up a little when the commander pressed the button to release the 432-pound Mk 44 torpedo at a position of 44°33'S, 64°16'W.

Splash!

Fortini couldn't see the torpedo's entry into the water, but he did see its parachute floating on the surface. The electronic brain of the torpedo, sensing that it had entered salt water, released its deployment parachute, and activated its 30 HP motor. To commence its spiral search, it began descending to a depth of 120 feet at 25 feet per second.

Contralmirante (Retired) Carlos Cal (left) and *Capitán de Fragata* (Retired) Enrique Fortini (right) holding a side profile print of an S-2E Tracker. Behind them is a painting, commissioned by *Capitán* Fortini, depicting his aircraft dropping a homing torpedo on 5 May 1982. The painting and the print were done by the aeronautical artist Carlos García. (Carlos García)

Above the surface, on board the aircraft, both the commander of the aircraft and the sonar operator heard, via the closest sonobuoy, the torpedo functioning correctly and the emission of its characteristic active sonar: "ping.... ping.... ping..." Moments later they could hear the pings double in frequency and the increase in revolutions of the weapon's propeller. At this moment the sonar operator started to sweat.

The reason for this was that the torpedo would only double its pings and increases its speed when its search changed into a hunt, that is to say, when it had locked onto its target. The sonar signals being received from the torpedo were those that the anti-submariners had learned in theory and had experienced so many times during training sorties. However, some minutes later, with the torpedo surely having exhausted its battery, no explosion had been heard. However, there was a change in the sounds coming from the sea as they stopped hearing the mechanical sounds across all the sensors they were monitoring. As Fortini recalled: "The sudden acoustic silence was extremely significant and absolutely unforgettable".

Having remained orbiting the area for a short spell, Fortini gained some height and then after a sweep of the radar, updated all the aircraft on the scene with the distance and bearing of the aircraft carrier. By now, both helicopters were short of fuel (a stationery hover rapidly empties the fuel tanks) and need to return to refuel. They both left immediately. Left alone, the Tracker was unable to regain the contact. Shortly after having refuelled at a base on the mainland, due to a lack of fuel to return directly to the carrier, it took off and headed back to "mother".

The remaining crews that flew that day were made up of *Capitán de Corbeta* Lorenzo, *Teniente de Fragata* Brandeburgo, *Suboficial Segundo* Carbone, *Teniente de Fragata* García, *Cabo Principal* Ramos (the last two did not want to get off 2-H-231) and *Cabo Principal* Premet on 2-H-231 and *Teniente de Fragata* Rey, *Teniente de Corbeta* Macaroni, *Cabo Principal* Sánchez, *Suboficial Segundo* Llanos and *Suboficial Primero* S. Álvarez on 2-H-234.

Teniente de Navío Enrique Fortini. He retired from the Argentine Navy as *Capitán de Fragata* and passed away in February 2013. (Enrique Fortini)

The relief helicopters took off with the remote hope of reacquiring the lost contact, and if not would at least continue to harass the submarine. According to the doctrine, these flights should not have taken place. Both helicopters, with enthusiastic but realistic crews on board, had a degraded tactical situation to deal with. They carried out, without success, both active and passive searches.

The submarine had got away.

The post-flight debrief was carried out with all the crews involved (four from the Sea Kings and two from the Trackers) and with various officers from the Carrier Air Wing and carrier staff. In addition, there was the participation of some officers that had experience in submarines such as *25 de Mayo* XO, *Capitán de Fragata* Ricardo Aumann, who had previously commanded submarine ARA *San Luis* and *Capitán de Corbeta* Daniel Geraci, who was the Submarine Assistant attached to the Fleet HQ.

Finally, it was decided that the contacts obtained should be classified as POSSUB Confidence 2/3.

There were opposing voices regarding the classification. Those who had participated in the missions were more prone to give it a higher classification while the higher-ranking officers who had followed the events from the carrier felt the confidence status was low and that the classification should reflect this.

Considering all of the new information that has come to light after the conflict, it's interesting to ask oneself if it is possible to determine if the contact that was attacked was a submarine or not. Certainly, the contact, in a basic analysis using merely a map, a ruler and a calculator, was behaving like a submarine. Even lacking the data that could be obtained by the analysis of the acoustic signature and the multiple contacts from various sensors, it should be emphasised that the average speed between the first contact at 0746 hrs and the second at 0910 hrs was approximately 11.5 knots. This is almost double the usual speed of a bowhead whale, found usually in the area. This speed is certainly coherent with a submarine in shallow waters that wished to remain stealthy, even when trying to escape a threat.

Likewise, the object moved, during its transit, from shallow to deeper waters. This coincides with what a submarine commander would do under the circumstances of being attacked – seek deeper water and increase speed to put more distance between itself and the search systems and weapons of its aggressor.

Here is a summary of the contact:

- Something resembling a submarine snorkel was observed on a calm sea by a qualified anti-submarine crew. This observation coincided with a small radar contact on the same bearing and distance.
- The contact was then gained by a Sea King by use of its dipping sonar. An especially valuable piece of information is that the contact maintained its bearing during the entire search until it changed course by 180º at a certain point when the helicopter had passed over its azimuth.
- The increasing in pings by the active sonar on the Mk 44 torpedo (which indicates that the torpedo has found an object that its pings are being returned by), bearing in mind the sea bed in the area of the attack is flat and sandy, is a strong indicator that the torpedo locked on to a target.
- The Tracker had eight separate contacts with its Magnetic Anomaly Detector. The object being detected was moving and had a course and speed that match those that were monitored by the sonar on the helicopter. Even though the MAD operator classified the object as "No MAD", this can be attributed to various reasons such as a poor calibration of the equipment or a low magnetic anomaly.

POSSUB Confidence 2/3 is not so adequate given the information above. PROBSUB Confidence 1 (as assigned by the Observer on the Sea King 2-H-231 during the search) would seem a much more appropriate rating.

Was HMS *Splendid* the contact attacked? That seemed, at first, to be the most logical conclusion. Indeed, of the three submarines in the war zone on 5 May (HMS *Conqueror*, HMS *Spartan* and HMS *Splendid*) the latter of the three was the closer one to the attack position. Likewise, this was the submarine that had been assigned to this patrol area.

Inside *Splendid*, at 0500 hrs on the 5th, the Navigation Officer had finished his calculations. He noted that they were at position 47º 37'S, 65º 06'W, level with Puerto Deseado. The weather could be considered to be good and the sea was calm with a light wind at the surface. Visibility was around 14,000 yards. Obviously, he didn't think there would be any layers (where there would be an abrupt change in temperature and salinity of the water around them). In areas of ocean with this depth it was unusual to find thermal layers.

The submarine was heading on a bearing of 225° (south-south-west) at a depth of 150 feet and a speed of nine knots. Without being aware of it, they were heading away from the Argentine Task Force. If the notes made by the navigator were accurate, they were about 130 miles away to the north.

The intention of the submarine's commander, Lane-Nott, was to return to Area Ricardo (The Argentine Navy had assigned secret code names to different zones of the ocean, something that the British had discovered within a very short time thanks to their intelligence services). After the previous bad day, they needed to redouble their efforts to find the aircraft carrier. He surely felt that the plaudits would all be given to his colleague on board HMS *Conqueror*, so it was necessary to get result to show to his superiors. Everything would change in a short time.

At exactly 0506 hrs, the sonar operator spoke up: "Conn, Sonar. Hold a new contact designated Sierra three-six. Bearing 230°. Two high frequency contact lines. Accompanied by a very noisy biological contact." He began to carefully monitor "S-36". According to his calculations, it was level with the Bahía de los Nodales in the Santa Cruz Province, a little to the south of the city of Puerto Deseado.

At 0700 hrs, after a prolonged plot, the XO finished his calculation of a firing solution. The target was sailing eastbound at a speed of seven knots. The distance to the target was 9,000 yards. Maybe the target was a cargo vessel, but to the sonarman monitoring the contact there was something that didn't quite seem right. Perhaps he had been thinking that this contact was the same one as the previous day, a few miles from Cabo Blanco (south of Golfo San Jorge), which had finally been classified as a submerged submarine.

At 0838 hrs, when the sun was shining off the surface of the sea, the sonarman noticed the unmistakable noise of a diesel engine, from contact S-36. This caused a small commotion in the sonar room, which increased when the blades of a propeller became audible at 0844 hrs: "Conn, Sonar. Contact Sierra three-six has one shaft with a four-bladed propeller. Bearing 272. Revolutions per minute – 124, Stopped!"

Just over half an hour later, considering the noises heard of control planes, clicks and bangs in the water, the contact was classified as a submerged conventional submarine. It could be, as noted by the commander, the same submarine that had been detected the previous day. It could also be the same contact that they detected in "Area Ricardo" on 1 May.

Lane-Nott ordered a fast move away from the area. They did not have any anti-submarine torpedoes loaded in their tubes, which therefore meant that they were unarmed in the face of the contact which was assumed to be hostile: there were no other British submarines in their area, and certainly no conventional diesel-electric ones.

At 0936 hrs the contact was reported to the north-north-east of their position at an updated approximate distance of 15,300 yards, navigating at a speed of 10 knots and a bearing of 140°. It was getting closer to *Splendid*. A short time later more metallic clicks were heard from the contact, and then at 0953 hrs the sonar informed that they had detected a faint burst of compressed cavitation and some harsh propeller blade flutter.

To an experienced submarine commander, these would have been unequivocal signs that they were dealing with a submarine, which was accelerating and changing depth.

Four minutes later, during a tense period inside *Splendid* (considering that the supposed enemy submarine was getting closer and adopting an attack posture), contact "S-36" was definitively lost. It was not detected again. A little time later (and a little more relaxed) Lane-Nott wrote:

> We have now had faint contact with a possible submarine contact on four occasions. In view of COR 202, suggesting that *Salta* may be patrolling off a Naval Base somewhere, intend (a) clearing the area and (b) drawing back the Mark 8 from 3 tube and replacing it with a Mk 24. If we get this contact again we will fire at it. My assessment is that S-36 was almost certainly a submarine but once again at

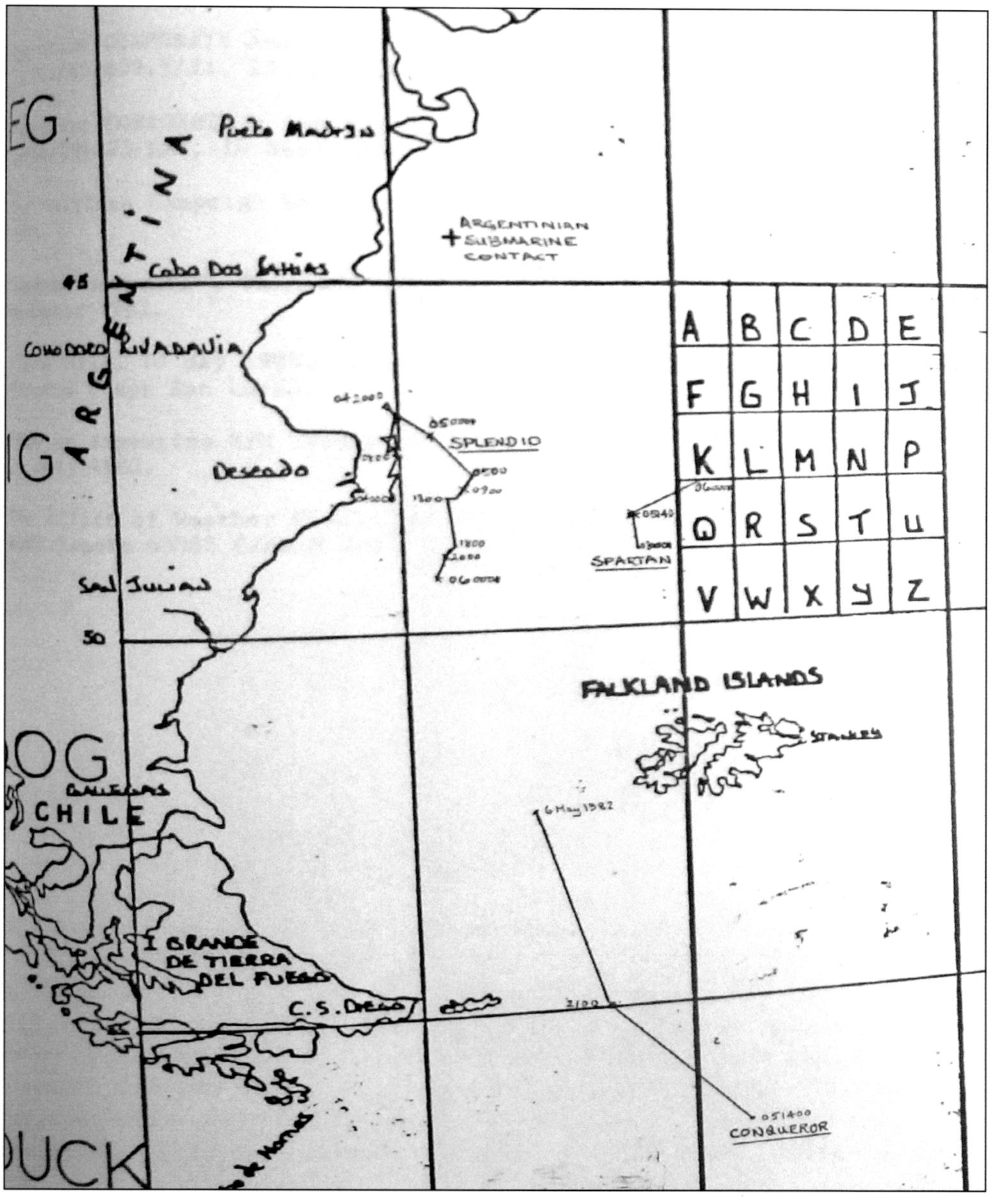

The Royal Navy's Submarine Track Plot – 5 / 6 May 1982. (Royal Navy)

A Zulu in the Falklands/Malvinas. Soviet submarine B-73 *Lira* alongside the *Mikhail Kalinin* in Port Stanley, February 1972. The islands were not immune to the Cold War and the Soviet presence. (D. Petterson)

Bell 212 H-88 of the Argentine Air Force. The photograph was taken in the afternoon of 5 May, from ARA *Cabo San Antonio*. (*Armada Argentina*)

very long range – 15 to 20,000 yards – perhaps even further.

It had been another tense day aboard *Splendid*.

Therefore, with this information to hand, HMS *Splendid* could not have been the contact attacked by the Argentines. The boat was very far south and, having detected a submerged submarine, was moving still further away from the area being transited by the aircraft-carrier. Neither was it HMS *Spartan* or HMS *Conqueror*. It is also important to remember that no other British submarine was permitted to enter the patrol area that was occupied by *Splendid*.

The contact that was attacked also could not have been Argentine. At the beginning of the conflict, the Argentine Navy had four submarines: ARAs *Santiago del Estero*, *Santa Fe*, *San Luis* and *Salta*. ARA *Santiago de Estero* had been out of service since 1981, although she had been moved towards Puerto Belgrano and hidden between two moored ships to deceive the British intelligence services.

ARA *Santa Fe,* as mentioned previously, had already been captured in South Georgia. The selfless and hard-working ARA *San Luís*, a modern Type 209 submarine was on that day carrying out a war patrol off the north coast of the Falklands/Malvinas Islands. Lastly, ARA *Salta*, as we have seen, thought to have been carrying out a patrol in Argentine coastal waters, was actually still in the Puerto Belgrano Naval Base undergoing urgent repairs[1].

So, we have the curious situation where, in the same area of operations, the Argentine forces believed that they had detected a British submarine, while at the same time the British believed that they had detected an Argentine submarine. Both sides were so convinced, that in one case the Argentines proceeded to attack the target, and in the other the British withdrew from the area due to a lack of an anti-submarine weapon being loaded.

There is a considerable distance (around 100 nautical miles) between Bahía Camarones (level with where the target was attacked by the Argentine Navy) and Bahía de los Nodales, where *Splendid* detected a submarine contact. Therefore, there must have been two submarines operating in that area on 5 May.

This is somewhat reminiscent of the two submarines detected and attacked by the Argentine Navy in the Golfo Nuevo in 1960, whose nationalities were never determined. Likewise, there are the two mysterious submarines attacked by the Chilean Navy in 1976 off the port of Valparaiso. In other words, maybe just a curious coincidence, each time a phantom submarine has appeared, so has another one.

It is also possible that these submarines were spotted from land in Caleta Olivia on 1 May at 1030 hrs, according to the war diary kept by the General Roca Military School in Comodoro Rivadavia[2]. This was coincidentally close to Area Ricardo, where one of the mysterious submarines was detected by HMS *Splendid*. It was perhaps also the one spotted at 0800 hrs on 4 May by the Argentine fishing vessel *Doña Mariela*, which sent by radio to the Argentine Navy: "Submarine spotted diving at latitude 45° 10'S, longitude 66° 00'W".

An Argentine Air Force Bell-212 helicopter (H-88, callsign *Liebre*) participating in a Search and Rescue sortie looking for ARA *Alferez Sobral*, reported having observed two submerged submarines, one larger than the other, near Puerto Deseado this same 5 May, at around 1000 hrs. The submarines, the crew reported, were 50 nautical miles from each other: *Splendid* and the ghost submarine?

Which country were they from? What were they doing there?

In the first place, it is unlikely that other nations' submarines would have found themselves in the war zone by mistake. Both navies involved in the conflict, as per standard western doctrines, had orders to attack, without warning, any submerged contact not identified as friendly units. This was known, having been communicated in either an explicit or inexplicit way to third-party countries that possessed submarines.

These countries, which would surely wish to avoid the danger of an accidental attack, proceeded to withdraw their submarines from the war zone, or stop them from heading in that direction in the first place.

USS *Parche*, circa 1979. (US Navy)

K-525 *Arkhangelsk*, an Oscar I class nuclear-powered cruise missile submarine of the Soviet Navy. According to unconfirmed information we received from a Russian submariner historian, this submarine followed the British fleet from 5 April to 21 May 1982. The official history of the submarine indicates that it was doing tests of 650/533 mm torpedoes and Granit/SS-N-19 missiles but in reality, he told us, it had been sent to the South Atlantic with orders, still secret to this day, to stalk the British Task Force. There is no independent document or testimony that corroborates this information. (US DoD)

For example, both the UK and Argentina alerted Brazil about the danger area. Not surprisingly, Brazil informed both belligerent nations that its submarines would not go any further than 200 miles from its coastline.

To date, no third country has officially admitted that its boats were operating near the islands. However, there are three countries that could have had a certain level of interest in monitoring the development of the conflict and/or the tactics employed.

Firstly, Chile should be considered. It possessed conventional submarines of the Oberon Class (like the British submarine HMS *Onyx*) and, it is worth recalling, during the first days of May that there were two reports of Oberon class submarines, easily recognised by their distinctive sonar dome situated on the top of the bow. The first took place on the afternoon on 5 May: an Oberon class boat manoeuvring to dive, some 100 miles to the north of San Carlos strait, was reported by an Argentine Navy observer on-board an Argentine Air Force Boeing 707 flying a reconnaissance mission. Furthermore, sightings of Oberons from land were also reported between Punta Tombo and Playa Union in the Chubut Province.

Having said that, it is perfectly possible to believe that the Oberon class submarines that were sighted were Chilean, especially bearing in mind the good relationship between Chile and the United Kingdom and the poor state of the relationship between the former and Argentina (to such an extent that the Chilean fleet and its submarines put to sea in complete radio silence on 22 April).

However, this can only be an assumption. In truth, this supposition does not correlate with any Argentine Naval Intelligence report, newspaper article or any other comment that has filtered out during the following years.

Secondly, we should consider the United States. At the time of the conflict, as today, it possessed the most efficient fleet of submarines in the world. It is known there were no South Atlantic patrols for its nuclear attack submarines nor for its ballistic missile submarines (SSBNs). Therefore, it is unlikely that a US Navy submarine would be around the conflict zone by chance. What has been possible to confirm

On 11 July 1982, Colonel Georgy Bul'bénkov was ordered to fly his Tu-95 (ASCC-code 'Bear-D'), belonging to 392 ODRAP (Soviet Navy, Naval Aviation), from Angola to a point in the middle of the Atlantic close to Ascension Island. His mission was to check any battle damage to carrier HMS *Hermes*, returning home from the South Atlantic War. Having located the carrier, and shortly before flying past it (*Hermes* was in close company of RFA *Tidespring*), his aircraft was intercepted and photographed by a Phantom FRG.2 (XV484) of 29 Sqn RAF, operating from RAF Wideawake. (Nigel Marks)

Another view of the same Tu-95. (Nigel Marks)

is that one had been close to the war zone during its transit from its base in the Pacific to the Barents Sea, via Cape Horn. USS *Parche* (SSN-683), a Sturgeon class nuclear-powered submarine modified for espionage missions, made this journey[3].

The assignment that it was undertaking, for which it received a Presidential Unit Citation following its 137-day mission, was to tap a submerged communications cable that linked two Soviet bases. Such a long and unusual route had been chosen (bearing in mind that the most direct path would have been under the Arctic) because the US Navy suspected a spy within its ranks. Therefore, this route was chosen to mislead the Soviet intelligence agencies.

This spy did, in fact exist, turning out to be John Anthony Walker Jr, a retired US Navy communications specialist who had, along with some other sailors recruited by him, been selling military secrets related to submarine warfare to the Soviet Union.

Therefore, some doubt will always remain as to whether some of these contacts could be due to USS *Parche* or some other US submarine.

The final nation that must be considered as a possible source of the submarine is the Soviet Union, which was in the middle of the Cold War against the western allies and at the time possessed the largest fleet of submarines in the world, which were considered their principal tool to deny the west the domination of the oceans.

The Soviet Navy did not have a patrol area in the South Atlantic

... and the Bear D crew also took pictures of the Phantom of Squadron Leader Russ Morley and Flying Officer Nigel Marks. (Soviet Navy)

either, except for the deployments to West Africa, which did have an 80 percent increase in 1982 when compared to the previous year. It's worth adding that the "West African patrol", with its base in Angola, in 1982 was carried out (along other surface units) by a conventional Foxtrot class submarine (during April/May the B-826, *Yaroslavsky Komsomolets*), an old but effective design from the 1950s[4].

At the same time, it must be borne in mind that, thanks to the espionage mission mentioned earlier, it is possible that there were Soviet submarines waiting for USS *Parche* in the waters around Cape Horn. In truth, this would have been the most logical place to intercept and then silently follow her, as the US submarine would have only been able to pass through the gap between the Tierra de Fuego and the permanent ice cap of Antarctica. Therefore, it is possible that Soviet submarines, seeking *Parche*, were the ones detected by the Argentine forces.

There is also a degree of logic that the Soviet Navy would have deployed submarines with the aim of evaluating one of NATO's members during a real shooting war. The war in the South Atlantic was an unbeatable opportunity for the Soviet Union to measure the capacities of its adversary and to aid the development of doctrine, tactics and technologies. Although the presence of its submarines was dismissed at the time by Moscow, what is undoubtedly true is that, in the middle of the Cold War, none of the adversaries showed off their true military capabilities to their rivals, and less still in the face of an intelligence operation being carried out.

It is not a secret that Soviet Tu-95RT long-range recce aircraft (NATO "Bear D") of the 392nd Independent Long-Range Reconnaissance Aviation Regiment, operating out of Luanda (Angola) overflew the British fleet on various occasions. The task of the Bears was critical because, as the conflict started, the Soviets lacked satellites that could follow the British fleet that had just sailed. Covering this gap in intelligence, the aircraft stationed in Angola flew more than 100 hours in April alone, in sorties that lasted up to 15 hours, gaining visual and electronic data from the Task Force.

The Soviets also assigned a spy ship to follow the Task Force (a Primorye class intelligence collector named *Zaporozhye*), tasked their fishing vessels to collect data and launched several satellites to cover the South Atlantic. This only goes to reinforce the theory regarding the level of Soviet interest in the British naval deployment that was taking place.

During the war there were various comments and reports by the British forces about the detection of at least one Soviet nuclear submarine, either in the waters around the Falklands/Malvinas or near Ascension Island. Perhaps the most obvious encounter happened on 11 May, when a Wessex helicopter from HMS *Antrim* detected and attacked a submerged contact evaluated as POSSUB, very far away from any Argentine submarine. According to its crew:

> ... although intelligence intimated that an Argentine threat was low in this area, the contact gained seemed to fit all the criteria for a submarine. Possibly it was a submarine from another Navy.

It must be noted that a British admiral (maybe too prudently) preferred not to return the nuclear depth charges the Royal Navy were armed with to the United Kingdom, in the face of the doubt that some Soviet submarine might decide to get involved in the conflict and help the Argentines.

Such rumours about the Soviet presence, with or without support, circulated and grew after the end of the conflict to such an extent that a Labour Member of Parliament (and a critic of the war, it must be said), with the aim of throwing doubt on the subject raised a concisely written question for the Prime Minister:

> Mr. Dalyell asked the Prime Minister what knowledge is available to Her Majesty's Government about the presence of a Soviet submarine in the vicinity of the Falkland Islands maritime exclusion zone on or about 1 May 1982.
>
> The Prime Minister: "It is not our practice to comment on submarine operations". (A reply given to Mr Tam Dalyell by the Prime Minister Margaret Thatcher as a written answer on 15 July 1985)

Destroyer ARA *Santísima Trinidad.* (*Armada Argentina*)

The reply by the Prime Minister is, at the very least, a clue. Was there really a suspicion of the presence of a Soviet nuclear submarine in the South Atlantic? The British Chief of Naval Staff argued during the war "that no one could be that categorical about the absence of Soviet submarines."

Other than this information, and the fact that the Soviet Union had an obvious interest in having at least a submarine in the area, there is no concrete evidence that permits us to assert the presence of Soviet boat during these days of May.

Furthermore, the US Navy, in its official reports that were classified Top Secret for years, indicate that it had not been able to detect any Soviet vessels in the waters around the Falklands/Malvinas during the war – but this, of course, does not say that there were not any there. In fact, the American report does not mention the visit of a Soviet nuclear boat (K-513, a Victor II class) to the waters around Ascension Island waters in November 1982, but it is a fact that that happened. The doubt, as seized upon by British MP Tam Dalyell three years after the war, persists to this day.

Therefore, it is a reasonable assumption that the phantom submarines were either Chilean, US, Soviet or maybe even from another Commonwealth country (for example the Royal Australian Navy had two Oberon class submarines at the time, HMAS *Onslow* and HMAS *Ovens*, that were specifically adapted for intelligence operations and which operated in such distant places such as the coasts of China and Libya.[5]).

Through an analysis of the information in the war diaries and logs, is it possible to come to a conclusion as to the identity of these submarines? From the data regarding the contacts made by HMS *Splendid*, it is known that:

- The submarine was snorkelling or on the surface (having started its diesel engines). This does not automatically mean that it is a conventional submarine. In fact, all nuclear-powered submarines have diesel engines installed in case of problems with their main power plant.
- It possessed at least one shaft with a four-bladed propeller. This doesn't necessarily indicate that it did not have two or more shafts, only that only one of them was detected and/or functioning at that moment.

The only thing that can be inferred from the submarine attacked by the Argentine Navy is that it was spotted snorkelling. It is not possible to make any conclusion from this piece of information.

Indeed, with respect to the contact detected in Bahía de los Nodales, of the three countries that we investigated, only the Chilean Balao class submarines (old sea wolves of the Second World War) have four bladed propellers. These submarines did not have a snorkel and had to come to the surface to recharge their batteries. But at that time, only the ARCH *Simpson* remained and it was more of a museum piece than a naval combat vessel. Such was the fact that it was retired from active service in the middle of 1982. All the other possible submarine types possessed propellers with more blades, from five upwards, which is the trend for more modern boats.

With the information collected, it is impossible to determine the type of submarine that was detected by *Splendid* nor that attacked by the Tracker. The only thing that we can be sure of is that their crews must have had a big shock: either detected by a British attack submarine or attacked by Argentine helicopters and aircraft. They must surely have taken home, wherever home might be, a great story to tell.

At the end of this day, *Splendid* informed Northwood HQ that it had problems in one of its turbo generators, as well as steam losses in its power plant and, for these reasons it was withdrawing "out of area to repair a major defect"[6]. At a critical moment, it abandoned the material objective it was pursuing, and significantly reduced the chances of success of neutralizing the Argentine aircraft carrier, a specific directive that the submarine force had received.

Returning to the account of Argentine operations on 5 May, the anti-submarine operations continued into the afternoon. Tracker 2-AS-22 was launched under the command of *Teniente de Navío* Julio "Negro" Garavaglia at 1330 hrs. The rest of the crew was made up by *Teniente de Fragata* Alvarez, *Suboficial Segundo* R. Lencina and *Suboficial Segundo* Vallejos. They carried out a LOFAR search without any apparent result. Before leaving the search area, they deployed a new line of eight-hour endurance sonobuoys, which were to be used by the next aircraft, and arrived back at the ship at 1745 hrs.

That relief aircraft was 2-AS-24, piloted by *Teniente de Navío* "Lince" Membrana (with *Teniente de Corbeta* "Rafa" Cornejo Sola, *Suboficial Segundo* I. Lencina and *Cabo Primero* Conde making up the crew), which was launched at 2355 hrs and monitored the line of sonobuoys to ensure the safe passage of the fleet and did not gain any contacts. They landed back on deck at 0500 hrs on 6 May.

During the afternoon of that same day, *Santísima Trinidad* was sent back to Puerto Belgrano due to banging noises coming from one of the propeller shafts (and the following day it was in a dry dock). It should also be remembered that *Py* was carrying out tasks in support of the *Sobral* and did not re-join the rest of the fleet until the last hours of the day.

Therefore, that afternoon, the only surface unit that was protecting the aircraft carrier was ARA *Hércules*. One warship and a handful of aircraft: a few braves protecting a giant.

8
6 MAY – STILL ON GUARD

> I am afraid I cannot go into much detail as I am still bound by the Official Secrets Act and a lot of what we were tasked with has never been made public. Needless to say we had long periods of quiet patrolling with short periods of drama (a crew member of HMS *Spartan*).

Before sunrise, at 0705 hrs, after a quick check over and refuelling, 2-AS-24 was catapulted off the ship again, now under the command of *Capitán de Corbeta* Dabini (with the rest of the crew made up of *Teniente de Fragata* Sanguinetti, *Suboficial Segundo* Vallejo and *Cabo Principal* Cravero). The Tracker's task was, once again, to deploy a sonobuoy barrier, this time in front of the naval formation.

As previously mentioned, night operations aboard the carrier were the exclusive domain of the Anti-Submarine Naval Air Squadron. As a result, the unit found itself busy at all hours, and as some of the squadron's personnel like to boast *"launching at night is only for real men"*. There was a reason why its unofficial nickname was "The Owls."

The day had terrible visibility and a cloud ceiling of only 1,000 feet. While flying in the cloud, at 0850 hrs, 2-AS-24 gained a small radar contact at a position 41°53' S, 63°03' W which was lost at about 2 miles whilst flying to investigate it.

Despite this, and without much expectation of sinking anything, an attack was carried out with depth charges, of which only one released and without any apparent results. The intention of the crew, with the previous day's events fresh in mind, was to continue harassing the British. However, there were not any enemy submarines in the location.

Although the area where the attack took place was previously reserved for *Splendid*, this had already (as stated before) reported various defects and for this reason had definitively abandoned its pursuit of the Argentine aircraft carrier, and at the time was sailing at a speed of 12 knots at a latitude of almost 50° south, "in order to avoid Argentine ASW air activity"[1] (as Northwood HQ ordered). It was, therefore, already quite a considerable distance from the location of the attack.

Much to Lane-Nott's disappointment, the British intelligence

The view from the pilot's seat on a S-2E Tracker on final approach to ARA *25 de Mayo*. (*Armada Argentina*)

Argentine Air Force Fokker F-27 Troopship TC-78. (Alejandro Amendolara)

Fokker F-27 Troopship alongside a C-130 Hercules, during an Argentine Air Force Open Day in the mid-eighties. (Alejandro Amendolara)

services had now pinpointed the location of *25 de Mayo* much further to the north of their position. He no doubt regretted the fact that they had to withdraw from the area of operations, but hoped that one of their other submarines would complete their yet incomplete task. He wrote the following in *Splendid´s* war diary:

> The main threat (CVA) is now assessed as being to the north. TU 324.1 (Spartan) is being stationed slightly further north. To withdraw for repairs to the port turbo generator and MS1/7 we would be best placed to retire to the east behind Spartan.

The last hurdle that the aircraft carrier and its escorts would have to face would be to get past the threat posed by the superbly manned HMS *Spartan*, possibly the most dangerous of the steel sharks which was still stalking the fleet.

Without being aware of any of this, *Capitán* Dabini's aircraft, with the customary assistance from the Landing Signal Officer (LSO), landed back on board without any serious problems at 0950 hrs.

As *Capitán* Dabini's Tracker touched down, the carrier was completely alone; its escorts had remained in the Golfo San Matías in an area that was deemed to be off limits to the British submarines due to its shallow waters. This was a false assumption.

Indeed, an Argentine Air Force Fokker F-27 transport aircraft, with the registration TC-78 (callsign "Titan"), carrying out a reconnaissance support mission for the Task Force, reported the sighting of a submarine at periscope depth at a position of 40º 15'S, 60º 15´W, 150 miles from Puerto Belgrano and some 30 miles behind the carrier, on a course of 190º.

The Argentine Navy and Air Force had coordinated a series of surface search sorties with the aim of detecting any possible threats to the naval surface units. These flights were carried out mainly by the twin-engined Fokker F-27s, an aircraft that was not appropriate for the maritime reconnaissance role but, of course, the Air Force didn't really possess any aircraft that were more suitable.

The idea was to do everything possible to avoid an intruder positioning itself in coastal waters (long-range reconnaissance tasks were being performed by the Air Force Boeing 707s), but the flights were sparse, the equipment not very suitable and the crews untrained in carrying out flights over water.

This flight, which had taken off from Viedma at 1400 hrs and was not due to return until 1845 hrs, was commanded by *Mayor* O. Botto with the rest of the crew made up of *Capitán* Carlos Romeo Filippi, *Capitán* Julio Mirgone and the NCOs Altamiranda, Seguí y Godoy.

The submarine had been spotted by the pilot, co-pilot and a crewman. During a second pass, carried out at a height of some 5,000 feet, the submarine had submerged, and it was possible to see the fin, periscope and the wake[2].

Because of this detection, a Sea King was launched from the carrier, some thirty minutes later, towards the datum. The crew of the F-27 was not qualified for the task of searching for submarines (which required special training), and a fruitless search by the helicopter ensued. During the helicopter's return to the carrier, its crew classified the sighting as NONSUB and were sure that the Air Force crew had made a blunder.

The Sea King's experienced Observer, again *Teniente* Edgardo García, recalled:

> In less than thirty minutes we had taken off in the Sea King, but we had our doubts about the sighting of this submarine as the crew were not trained on how to classify submarine sightings. For this reason, and as we searched and found nothing, the sighting by the Air Force was rejected, stating that they had probably seen a whale.

Argentine Type 209 submarine ARA *Salta*. (*Armada Argentina*)

Without devaluing the crew of the Fokker, the Navy crew had good reason for thinking this way, as during times of peace and during exercises there had been innumerable cases of detections which later turned out to be whales, reflections, waves and even magnetic anomalies in the Earth – all of which to the human eye or the aircraft sensors appeared to be a submarine.

These false sightings had multiplied during the conflict. For this reason, only personnel specifically trained in anti-submarine operations were permitted to classify a sighting as a CERTSUB. Additionally, it did not help the credibility of the report by the crew of "Titan" flight that they radioed insistently to the aircraft carrier *Independencia* (which was the name of previous fleet carrier to *25 de Mayo*) requesting the immediate launch of A-4Q fighter bomber aircraft…to attack a submarine.

The Fokker would later continue its flight to the access channel for Bahía Blanca (near the main Argentine naval base), where it reported another submarine, this time remarking that it was of a smaller size and a different colour.

To the surprise of everybody, the sighting that they reported was the Argentine Navy submarine ARA *Salta*, which was on its way to its final work-up mission, prior to its planned deployment to the war zone.

Because of this sighting, the Fokker crew was automatically qualified in anti-submarine warfare; therefore, their initial sighting immediately gained more credibility. For this reason, it was decided, therefore, to reclassify their "false" sighting as a certain submarine, or CERTSUB.

Consequently, ARA *Salta* was immediately ordered to return to port and the Tracker Squadron was tasked with another anti-submarine sortie.

At 1850 hrs Tracker 2-AS-24 (under the command of *Capitán de Corbeta* Goitía) took off and headed to the datum, where it dropped a field of seven sonobuoys which it then monitored without anything of note until 2330 hrs, at which point it headed back to the aircraft carrier. This aircraft was then relieved by 2-AS-26, which had taken off also at 2330 hrs and monitored the same sonobuoys without incident, and then a newly laid field, before landing back on deck at 0441 hrs.

Tracker 2-AS-24 was then launched once more into a murky dawn the following morning, taking off at 0540 hrs under the command of *Teniente de Navío* Garavaglia (with *Teniente de Fragata* "Chelo" Alvarez, and NCOs Lencina and Vallejos) for another anti-submarine search from an updated datum (now 40°16' S, 60°05'W), without obtaining any results before finally landing at 1040 hrs. For this search, a new pattern of sonobuoys was sown.

It is interesting to note the sonobuoy fields were laid to the east of the submarine sighting, on the assumption it would attempt to head for deeper waters, based on the operational experience gained the day before.

Unfortunately for the squadron, although the area covered was increased in line with the farthest that it could have possibly moved (Farthest-on-Circle), no submarine was detected by the time the operations were terminated at 2230 hrs on the 7th, with the Trackers having flown 11 hours in addition to several hours of the Sea King.

The contact that had been detected was in the area allocated to HMS *Spartan*. But the submarine had not yet arrived, making this contact another ghost of the war. A big, black, submerged ghost.

HMS *Spartan* (S105), under the command of Commander James Taylor, was, like HMS *Splendid*, a modern nuclear-powered attack submarine of the Swiftsure class that had entered service in 1979 and finally retired in 2006.

This submarine was one of the first vessels to head to the South Atlantic, leaving on 1 April. Forty-eight hours earlier it had been participating in the annual *Springtrain* exercises in the Mediterranean along with other ships that would later head south to the conflict. It was ordered to head for Gibraltar and take on provisions and weapons, which were obtained from the Oberon class submarine HMS *Oracle*. From there it headed south, maintaining a speed of 23 knots.

On arrival at the Area of Operations, it was ordered to patrol around the islands. It had the opportunity to observe, on 14 April, the mining of the waters surrounding the capital of the islands by both the *Forrest*, a small ship commandeered in the islands, and ARA *Islas de los Estados*, but did not receive orders to attack them.

It is interesting to consider that during this operation, the *Forrest* created a crescendo of noise with all the engines running, the crew hitting the bulkhead with hammers, chains hanging over the side, etc., to confuse a possible acoustic torpedo that could be launched at the other ship, which was at the time laying the minefield. Clearly, it was considered the British submarines would plot a firing solution based solely on sonar information and that any torpedoes launched would be acoustic homing ones.

With this mission given to the *Forrest*, the Argentine naval command displayed certain defeatism in the anti-submarine task, this

HMS *Spartan*, a Swiftsure class submarine. (Royal Navy)

Enemy air activity (Tracker and Bandeirante) detected by ESM. Water clarity and white sandy bottom in shallow water combine to limit daytime operations. Plan is to probe into shallower water by night, searching in deeper water by day.

HMS *Spartan* might consider itself to be somewhat fortunate as it had been operating in such shallow waters and managed to return home without so much as a scratch on it. Indeed, the submarine had been limited in its ability to move and stalk its prey.

This was due to the airborne vigilance in the Area of Operations, something that Commander Taylor was perfectly aware of, given that his ESM equipment did not stop receiving radar signals whenever it was deployed. Had HMS *Spartan* been operated in a careless way in front of the enemy, surely it would have been detected more times, and possibly attacked. In other words, the submarine had to operate with its "head down" and that made it possible for *25 de Mayo* pass through its patrol area on its way back to the north without any interference.

If HMS *Spartan* had not been restricted in its performance and patrolling, surely it would have detected the Argentine battle group and possibly could have sunk *25 de Mayo*. That this did not happen is not down to chance, but to the anti-submarine operations carried out.

attitude came about assuming that any nuclear-powered submarine could not be detected, and one could only try to minimise the success of an attack. Obviously, in that war stage, it could not be foreseen that the British submarines would carry out visual attacks with straight run torpedoes!

As previously mentioned, on 1 May it was ordered to search for *25 de Mayo*, being informed that it was some 100 miles from its position, but the commander was prevented from heading towards the target as it was in the sector assigned to HMS *Splendid*. On 6 May it was heading near Bahía Blanca, an area previously prohibited for it as it was in the "box" assigned to the now broken-down HMS *Splendid*. To fill the space left by the submarine withdrawn due to mechanical problems, HMS *Spartan* had moved in a few days from a patrol area to the north of the islands to the waters close to Puerto Belgrano Naval Base (near the Bahía Blanca city). In its Report of Proceedings, the commander of the submarine wrote:

> 6 May. Circumnavigated fishing fleet while sprinting to new patrol area in Bahía Blanca, south east of Puerto Belgrano…Cleared water to permit SPLENDID to pass eastbound to the south of me.

However, something that had been worrying Commander Taylor was whether his submarine could be visible from the air. Indeed, the conditions of the sea bed and the transparency of the water in the area allocated increased the possibility that an attentive observer could spot HMS *Spartan*, in the same way the CERTSUB was located by the Fokker. For that reason, on 8 May he wrote:

> ASVW (anti-surface vessel warfare) patrol in Bahía Blanca...

For its part, the Second Helicopter Naval Air Squadron carried out various flights moving personal and cargo this day, and the following days. However, what really irritated the crews were the missions as "radar decoys". This consisted of positioning the helicopter up-threat with the aim of seducing an enemy sea-skimming anti-ship missile with the helicopter, so that it did not lock onto one of the ships. It was necessary to fly at very low level and at thirty knots, pretending to be a surface unit. As soon as a missile was spotted, it was necessary to quickly increase height, with the knowledge that the missile would not be able to match the sudden increase in altitude. According to one of the Sea King pilots:

> We had to behave like a surface unit. If we spotted a missile and we saw it coming towards us, we had to wait till the last moment and climb abruptly. Nobody was sure if these theories would work, so the joke was that they would fly with the cabin doors on either side of the helicopter open, so that they would not be in any danger as the missile would just fly in one side of the helicopter and out of the other. (Oscar Brandeburgo)

Further to this anecdote, it is worth mentioning how scarce the anti-submarine resources were, bearing in mind all the different tasks being performed, which severely limited their availability. This did not go down well with the crews, all of them perfectly aware that by carrying out these other tasks, it was affecting the anti-submarine protection of the fleet.

9
7 MAY – MORE DEPTH CHARGES

> As for whether we felt threatened by anti-submarine aircraft the answer is always yes. A wise submariner always considers the airborne threat the most severe – even from an inexperienced navy such as the Argentine Navy. ("Jonty" Powis, HMS *Conqueror*)

On 7 May, with the British frustration at being unable to deal another decisive blow at sea, the Total Exclusion Zone was extended to the 12-mile territorial limit of continental Argentina. This meant that Argentine ships could be attacked and sunk whilst at sea even if they posed little direct threat to the British Task Force.

That did not seem to matter much to the sailors on board the aircraft carrier, with 2-AS-26 being launched into the reduced visibility and low cloud base under the command of *Teniente de Navío* Fortini with *Teniente de Corbeta* "Rafa" Cornejo Solá up front alongside him, and with NCOs I. Lencina and Conde behind them.

The sortie began without much in the way of incident. However, at 2010 hrs the radar operator gained a small radar contact at 42°31' S, 62°05' W and alerted the commander immediately.

The operator lost the contact at 11 miles, but regardless the aircraft continued to the datum and dropped a passive sonobuoy. As per doctrine, the acoustic operator tuned into the frequency and began listening to the audio signal coming from the buoy for about 30 seconds to confirm that it was functioning correctly. At this moment he thought that he could hear the beat of a propeller and the hum of a turbine, although these noises quickly weakened.

Without pausing to give it much thought, *Teniente* Cornejo Solá, as requested by the aircraft commander, released a depth charge from the aircraft which then detonated with a bang when reached the preselected depth.

Obviously, they weren't exactly within the established launch parameters for dropping a depth charge, but it was an opportunity to let the submarine know of their willingness to go on the offensive, and this opportunity was not to be missed.

This decision, of course, exceeded any of the conventional doctrine, but the Fortini – Cornejo Solá partnership was anything but conventional. The confidence they had in each other was based on a curious incident that had happened the previous year, when there still was a high level of tension between Argentina and the neighbouring country of Chile.

In that year Fortini had been the Intelligence Officer of the Aeronaval Anti-Submarine Squadron and had as one of his main tasks to record the acoustic signature of Chilean submarines. Knowing that one of these submarines would be operating in the waters of the Beagle Channel, the squadron designed a small invention that became known as the mini-SOSUS (SOSUS was a very advanced warning system based on listen devices on the sea floor, operated by the US Navy). The mini-SOSUS was a far humbler device: just a sonobuoy connected to a battery from a Fiat 600 car and deployed by hiding it in some seaweed on the shore.

Therefore, the operating life of the sonobuoy was multiplied many times and would allow the hidden operation of the buoy, in order to attempt to record a Chilean submarine's acoustic signature. This was a good example of "*ingenio criollo*" (an Argentine expression for an improvised solutions) used in anti-submarine warfare.

The device was placed in a strategic location and at night a Tracker aircraft would arrive at the local Ushuaia Naval Air Station and be quickly hidden in a hangar. On the roof of the hangar was an improvised aerial that allowed the aircraft inside to monitor the sonobuoy from a great distance while a generator supplied power to the Tracker. The device produced the required results and the acoustic signature was successfully recorded.

Nevertheless, a few days later, a Chilean commando team landed by boat on the beach where the device was hidden and stole it. *Teniente* Fortini was furious. How could they steal the "mini" from under our noses?

The revenge would come on the Chilean "Day of Naval Glories" on 21 May. A routine Tracker sortie would have Fortini and Cornejo Solá sitting side by side. The plan was simple. The commander quickly convinced first the co-pilot and then the rest of the crew. They soared the Tracker past Colmillos de Navarino Mountains, descended to low level and then flew past the parade taking place in the Chilean Naval base at Puerto Williams, on the other side of the disputed Beagle Channel, at scarcely 30 feet and then made a low-level escape. Of course, the salute would not go unnoticed by the neighbours. The response to this gentlemanly stunt was some badly aimed anti-aircraft fire and a more formal protest note:

> 1981 was an unforgettable year which even included an unexpected visit from the Chief of Naval Operations, who came to ask for my version of events. The Chilean Foreign Secretary had sent an angry diplomatic note to his Argentine counterpart due to a flypast that a Tracker had made of the parade ground at the Puerto Williams Naval Base at the precise moment they were celebrating their "Day of Naval Glories" and at an excessively low level. (Enrique Fortini)

After so many experiences together, why not push the boundaries a bit more and drop a depth charge? Maybe it was with that anecdote in the back of his mind, the commander of 2-AS-26 hooked back onto *25 de Mayo* to end that day's operations.

No British submarines were near the depth charge. HMS *Spartan* was a bit further to the north, while its sister, HMS *Splendid*, was still heading east and at that moment on the same meridian as the capital of the islands. Its commander, Lane-Nott, did not want to use its diesel engines (which would have required exposing its snorkel) and less still transit on the surface, even though he was in an area where there was minimal Argentine air activity. They managed to carry out the necessary repairs to *Splendid* a couple of days later near 48° 00'S, 44° 09'W. Either he was being very cautious, or he had acquired a prudent respect for the anti-submarine capacity of the Argentine Navy.

It's clear that the explosion of the depth charge would not have been detected by *Splendid*. But the charge would surely have been heard by those on-board *Spartan*. And no doubt they would have instinctively ducked their heads as a result. Courtesy of the Argentine Navy.

10
8 MAY – HMS *ONYX*?

Much of the patrol comprised surveillance operations amongst the myriad of islands which make up the Falklands. Frequently, the only sign of life would be a few sheep on the bare hillsides. Even finding features on which to take bearings for navigational fixes was a challenge. This led to a new notation in the log book – 'TOYAH'- standing for "top of yet another hill". The old adage about "...99% unadulterated boredom interspersed with 1% sheer terror" was certainly true in our case. (Andy Johnson, HMS *Onyx*)

On 8 May, at 0931 hrs, Tracker 2-AS-24 was catapulted off the flight deck under the command of *Capitán de Corbeta* Alberto Dabini, with the remainder of the crew made up of *Teniente de Fragata* Sanguinetti, *Cabo Principal* Paulinkas and *Cabo Primero* Cufre. Their task was to provide anti-submarine support between the 39° S and 44° S parallels and the 9° W and 60° W meridians. However, the sortie passed without incident.

Later in the day, at 1718 hrs, 2-AS-26 was launched into the air with a crew consisting of *Capitán* "Checho" Goitía, *Teniente de Corbeta* Pascual, *Suboficial Segundo* Vallejos and *Cabo Principal* Cravero, to carry out a surface reconnaissance flight. It was really the first day for nearly a week that the May sun had shone brightly.

After a sortie without, so far, any incident, at 1915 hrs the radar operator reported a small fading contact at 42°00'S, 61°11'W. Given the characteristics, it was classified as a POSSUB confidence 1, but the contact could not be regained. At this moment, 2-AS-26 was running short on fuel and for this reason had to break off and return rapidly to the carrier without being able to investigate. In the first few hours of the following day, 2-AS-22 was launched to look around the datum, but the meteorological conditions prevented this from taking place.

The 8th of May was also the day that, according to some accounts, HMS *Onyx* was damaged. HMS *Onyx* (S21), under the command of Lieutenant Commander Andrew Johnson, was, according to the official history, the only conventional British submarine that took part in operations in the Falklands/Malvinas conflict.

It was the last of the thirteen Oberon class submarines to be built for the Royal Navy, an improved version of the Porpoise class. It was commissioned in 1967 and was retired in 1991. It's worth mentioning that the Oberon class was, in its time, considered to be one of the quietest diesel/electric submarines in the world.

With an average displacement of 2,410 tonnes when submerged and of a relatively small size, the Oberons were an excellent platform for operating in littoral waters, to which HMS *Onyx* was especially suited, as it had undergone various refurbishments over the years to improve its fit out as a Special Forces submarine. The submarine's armament consisted of six torpedo tubes in the bow, which could launch either old Mk 8 straight-run torpedoes or the newer Tigerfish. Also, *Onyx* had a further two torpedo tubes in the stern, loaded with Mk 20S passive-seeker battery-powered torpedoes.

HMS *Onyx* left Gosport on 25 April, although it had to return briefly that evening to unload a sick crew member. It spent the week before it left provisioning and fitting out for carrying out Special Forces insertions, which included fitting brackets for machine guns on the fin[1], which was quite unusual for a modern submarine.

Once on its way, most of the voyage to Ascension Island was carried out on the surface at a maximum speed of 12 knots (and 18 submerged), taking approximately two weeks to reach these islands. Once there, they had to fix various mechanical issues with the engines as well as sealing a fuel leak. During this stop, they also refuelled from the RFA *Tidespring*, embarked a party made up of SBS men as well as various electronic warfare specialists, pushing the number on board up to 84, compared to a normal crew of 45 men.

From then on, their submersions would become more and more prolonged. It was during this part of the trip between Ascension and the Falklands/Malvinas where the submarine was spotted by an Argentine Air Force Boeing 707. As sailor Martin Clarke remembered:

> We were overflown by what I believe was an Argentine 707 reconnaissance plane and this caused us to dive as fast as we could.

He was right. The aircraft had been a Boeing 707 (with the registration TC-92 and callsign "Tronco"), under the command of *Vicecomodoro* Jorge Riccardini, who at 1116 hrs on 21 May reported the sighting of a submarine in the position 35° 23'S, 43° 44'W. As the co-pilot of the aircraft, *Mayor* Antonio Buira, remembered:

> On 21 or 22 May, whilst flying in the area between the Malvinas Islands and Ascension at some 1,200 miles from Buenos Aires we spotted what we thought was a small oiler below... but we were suspicious of this ship because it didn't have a flag and we couldn't see anyone on board, and I said to the commander that I thought it was a tactical refuelling ship. After overflying the ship and continuing for a while without any incidents we began to climb again, and the commander told me that he could see some waves that were being cut through very strangely and I immediately thought that it could be a submarine. We made a turn to the right and while descending

HMS *Onyx* running on the surface. The photograph was taken on 21 May from an Argentine Air Force Boeing 707 aircraft during a naval reconnaissance sortie. The submarine dived shortly after this picture was taken. (*Fuerza Aérea Argentina*)

we clearly saw a submarine navigating on the surface.

HMS *Onyx*, given its lack of speed, something not at all unusual for conventional submarines, did not arrive in the Area of Operations, some eight thousand miles from its home base, until approximately a month after its departure. Once in the South Atlantic, the submarine participated in various reconnaissance missions and landed an SBS team in the islands.

The interesting fact is that *Onyx* was not as independent from the surface fleet as its nuclear-powered sisters. According to Andy Johnson, *Onyx*'s CO:

Part of the crew of Argentine Air Force Boeing 707 TC-92 callsign *"Tronco"* (Log) during the sortie on 21 May 1982. This crew sighted HMS *Onyx* running on the surface. (via Eduardo Daghero)

> Any rendezvous to collect personnel and equipment, or obtain a briefing, took place at night. Before the submarine could surface, we had to establish the identity of our escort, generally in pitch darkness and rough seas without the assistance of radar. Once on the surface, *Onyx* would set off on a mad dash behind the escort. Freezing, salt-laden air funnelling down the conning tower and through the boat to feed the roaring diesels was everywhere. There was then the tricky business of getting alongside a darkened ship that could only be seen with the naked eye from a few tens of yards. The first attempt was rarely successful. We arrived at briefings numbed, swaddled in layers of coats and sweaters, blinking like moles in the bright light. On one occasion, a well-known and frequently quoted correspondent witnessed our arrival. So much for secrecy we thought – but the ensuing silence in the media indicated a suitably Nelsonian eye had been adopted! All work had to be finished in time for an equally frantic and freezing dash back to the obscurity of the open ocean before daylight.

During a Special Forces mission that took place on 5 June, in waters south of Cape Meredith (Cabo Belgrano), and before disembarking members of the SBS near Chatham Harbour, the submarine suffered damage to the bow and keel which led to two torpedoes becoming trapped in their launch tubes, and were only finally removed on the submarine's return to the UK. Andy Johnson:

> An effort to complete a reconnaissance mission at short notice nearly ended the patrol. Many of the charts used to navigate in those waters had not changed significantly since James Cook had first drawn them. The occasional soundings he made at that time were undoubtedly adequate for his small sailing vessel. They scarcely matched the requirements of 2,500-ton submarine two centuries later. In consequence, *Onyx* discovered an uncharted pinnacle of rock in a most dramatic fashion – by running in to it whilst dived. Although everyone reacted admirably, and control was quickly regained, it is probably safe to say the only people on board who appeared really calm were our 'guests' from special forces. Not entirely due to their steel nerves – no-one had time to explain to them what had happened!

The damage did not cause major problems for the submarine, which finished its war patrol of 117 days with a degree of normality, which included on the 21 June, as mentioned elsewhere, the sinking of the remains of LSL *Sir Galahad*.

However, Argentine sources on many occasions have written that the submarine could have been damaged through various actions carried out by Argentine naval units; that this "navigational chart error" never took place and that is only an excuse.

They claim that on at least three occasions it could have been damaged. The first of these was detailed earlier in this book, when the events of 5 May were analysed. On this occasion, the Argentine Navy communicated to its units shortly after the events unfolded the contact that had been attacked was HMS *Onyx*.

Another occasion was on 8 May. The Argentine submarine ARA *San Luis* was trying to identify a faint contact when the sonar operators heard a strange noise in the stern sector which was quickly evaluated as a possible torpedo. Trying to avoid the weapon's lock, the submarine was forced to make evasive manoeuvres and to drop countermeasures.

Upon regaining the contact, and after sonar ruled out the possibility of marine life producing it, its commander concluded it was a submarine on approach. At 2142 hrs he ordered the firing of a Mk 37 mod. 3 torpedo, and a detonation was heard sixteen minutes later on the target's bearing, possibly after the torpedo striking the sea floor. No secondary explosions were detected, and the sonar operators lost the contact after the detonation[2].

Some sources, without any detail, point towards HMS *Onyx* being also the target of the attack, which post war analysis have suggested could have really been shoals of fish.

They have claimed that it was also the target attacked by ARA *Bouchard*, an old former-US Navy Allen M. Sumner-class destroyer that on 16 May took part in an action which, for its peculiar characteristics merits explanation in greater detail.

On the night of 15 May, the destroyer, along with ARA *Piedrabuena* (another Sumner-class ship), was anchored two miles from the Argentine coast around Rio Grande in the Tierra del Fuego, providing protection to its Naval Air Base which, amongst other things, was home to the Super Etendards and their deadly Exocet missiles.

The ship was alert and well stocked with ammunition for its 5" and anti-aircraft guns. It also had all its Exocet MM-38 missiles and regarding anti-submarine weaponry, had two Mk44 and three A244/S torpedoes (loaded on triple Mk 32 Surface Vessel Torpedo Tubes), six Mk 9 Depth charges and 538 Hedgehog mortar rounds.

In these circumstances, the characteristic ping of an active sonar was detected and later, the same noise repeated and could be heard,

HMS *Onyx* in dry dock, showing the damage to the bow torpedo tubes. (via Andrew Johnson)

without any special equipment, by crew members of the ship that were located below the ship's waterline. As remembered by sailor Adalberto (Beto) Alvarez:

> Being in the aft deck, from time to time we heard this noise. The silence of the night and because the ship was anchored made the sound more noticeable.

As there were no other ships in the area, the only possible source of this sound was a submarine.

An alternative explanation was that the destroyer crew heard the energy sound wave emitted by an echo sounder device, which is like an active sonar and measures the depth of the water beneath a vessel (in a similar way to a radio altimeter) to avoid collisions. Regarding the scarcity of reliable information about the sea floor in the zone, the navigating officer on HMS *Conqueror*, "Jonty" Powis recalled the intensive use of that piece of equipment during the Falklands/Malvinas conflict:

> We operated with echo sounder continuously and rehearsed slowing down, coming shallow and reversing course in one motion. We met several pinnacles for which that drill proved a life saver.

It is thought possible, therefore, that other submarines in the area, that similarly lacked reliable information about the sea floor, as HMS *Conqueror* did, had decided to use the same equipment, which may be the sounds that the crew of *Bouchard* heard – a working echo sounder.

Next day (16 May) at 1910 hrs, during dense fog and after a brief scan with the radar (the radar was turned on sporadically to not give away their position) a solid contact was gained at 3,000 yards, along with three smaller echoes which were assumed to be a submarine and small craft typically used by Special Forces[3]. As sailor Alvarez recalled:

> The radar, despite the differences in technology with the modern British sets, worked well. For this reason, *Bouchard* had won the recent prize for fire control radar in the fleet and this accomplishment at least boosted the moral of the crew at the time when we had to advance towards the British.
>
> Following hearing the sonar noises and the negative contact on the surface, some hours later, on doing another scan with the radar, a solid contact emerged on the screen, quickly followed by three small points which had the characteristic shape, at least to radar operators, of a "V" that was typical of rubber boats powered by outboard motors. From this point they set out towards the continental coast in coordinated movement. The attention of

Submarine Weapons. Falklands/Malvinas 1982

Weapon	Type	Guidance System	Target	Warhead Weight (lb)	Operational range (yards)	Submarine
SST-4	Torpedo	Wire-guided. Passive sonar capability	Anti-ship	573	12,000 at 35 knots / 40,000 at 23 knots	ARA *San Luis* / ARA *Salta*
Mk 37 mod. 3	Torpedo	Gyroscope (initial) passive (cruise) and active sonar (terminal)	Anti-ship / Anti-submarine	330	10,000 at 26 knots / 23,000 at 17 knots	ARA *San Luis* / ARA *Salta* / ARA *Santa Fe*
Mk 14	Torpedo	Gyroscope	Anti-ship	643	4,500 at 46 knots / 9,000 at 31.1 knots	ARA *Santa Fe*
Mk 8 mod. 4	Torpedo	Gyroscope	Anti-ship	805	5,000 at 45.4 knots / 7,000 at 41 knots	HMS *Spartan* / HMS *Splendid* / HMS *Conqueror* / HMS *Valiant* / HMS *Courageous* / HMS *Onyx*
Mk 24 mod. 0	Torpedo	Wire-guided. Passive and active sonar capability	Anti-submarine	295	14,000 at 35 knots / 31,600 at 24 knots	HMS *Spartan* / HMS *Splendid*
Mk 24 mod. 1	Torpedo	Wire-guided. Passive and active sonar capability	Anti-ship / Anti-submarine	295	14,000 at 35 knots / 31,600 at 24 knots	HMS *Conqueror* / HMS *Valiant* / HMS *Courageous* / HMS *Onyx*
Mk 20S	Torpedo	Passive sonar	Anti-submarine	196	12,000	HMS *Onyx*
Royal Navy Sub Harpoon	Missile	Inertial / Active radar	Anti-ship	488.5	75 nautical miles	HMS *Courageous*

Destroyer ARA *Bouchard*. (*Armada Argentina*)

Bouchard focused on these contacts and the larger object began to get smaller.

While the ship's commander ordered the anchor to be raised and set off toward these contacts, they open fire with the two twin 5" gun-turrets on the bow of the ship, observing as the large contact disappeared finally from the radar and the remaining small contacts changed course by 180° and headed out to sea. Once more Alvarez recalled:

> Because of all of this, we once again manned the anti-submarine positions. An NCO manned the Hedgehog launcher on the starboard side and I, along with three other lads, manned the depth charge cages at the stern. When the ship began to turn and get underway, I asked what was happening and they told me that they were going to open fire on some targets that were heading for the coast. While we made for the nearest cargo hatch, one of our shipmates located on the bow was hit by the blast wave from the first salvo, which flung him against a hatch and left him winded.

The firing stopped shortly afterwards, partly as *Bouchard* had lost the contact but also not to cause damage to the *Piedrabuena* which was also on its way to the datum. A thorough search of the area did not find anything, and the contact could not be followed due to deficiencies in the sonar of the destroyer.

Their sonar equipment had not been functioning properly since 2 May, and in any case the passive sonar rarely produced very good results. For example, when they were sailing in the company of *General Belgrano*, they were able to detect the noisy cruiser only at some 4,000 yards.

This incident should be seen in the same frame as a Special Forces operation called "Plum Duff", the clearest evidence of this being the discovery of a destroyed British Sea King (ZA-290) near Punta Arenas in Chile. Its objective was to monitor the Naval Airbase at Rio Grande and, if the opportunity arose, to attack with the aim of killing the Super Etendard pilots and destroying their missiles and aircraft. It would not be wild, therefore, to imagine that there was a submarine in this area of operations, as much to land troops as to provide a possible means of escape. However, it has been insisted the possible target was *Onyx*, a claim which was only reinforced with the damaged suffered to its bow as "irrefutable" evidence.

Now, the speed of the Oberon class submarines is not exactly a secret. With that in mind and calculating an average speed of 10 knots during its journey south (including provision for stops to refuel and carry out maintenance) *Onyx* could never have been in that area of operations on the occasions mentioned above.

But, according to its CO, talking about *Onyx* being the "most attacked boat in the war": "it's interesting to know that we attracted so much attention from the Argentine side – seems to make that long trip somehow worthwhile!"

11
FINAL CURTAIN

> Not a single British unit successfully achieved contact on the CVA, *25 de Mayo*, throughout Operation Corporate. (Admiral Peter Herbert, Flag Officer Submarines)

On the morning of 9 May the aircraft carrier was located close to the city of Viedma, inside territorial waters, sailing in circles at slow speed and with the intermittent company of its escorts, which every now and again had to break off to go and refuel. It was clear that it was not going to be possible to take advantage of any tactical situation in the immediate future, which was why, with an ever-increasing number of material defects, it was decided was decided to sail *25 de Mayo* into Puerto Belgrano.

The carrier was therefore ordered to head north at its maximum possible speed. When it reached the border of Buenos Aires Province between 1557 hrs and 1637 hrs, its A-4Q and Sea Kings were dispatched to Espora and at 1955 hrs local time, the carrier joined up with ARA *Py* to facilitate coordinating their entry into the access channel to the naval base. During the first hours of the 10 May it launched its Tracker aircraft and, at 0430 hrs it radioed that it had entered the channel.

Having finally entered port, the carrier could now be safe from attack. It moored alongside the main pier at 0850 hrs and shortly after the crew began to disembark. The members of the Carrier Air Wing which had remained on board did the same. However, the war was not yet over for most them.

The arrival of the aircraft carrier to Puerto Belgrano was the end of its journey and was a small operational success, not properly recognised, for the whole of the Argentine Navy which must be a matter of pride for all those involved in its protection.

The manoeuvre should be framed within the strategic framework that demanded the return of the fleet to safe waters. This was a reasonable decision, as can be read in later objective analysis carried out by prestigious experts in naval warfare, amongst them Captain Wayne Hughes Jr of the US Navy in his book "Fleet Tactics and Coastal Combat" which arrived at the conclusion that, certainly, on an open sea, a fleet that is inferior to its opponent (as the Argentine fleet was in comparison with the British one) would generally be destroyed by an enemy only slightly superior, which would also suffer less damage in any engagement. It is for this reason it is stated the Argentine Navy acted correctly at a strategic level by withdrawing to territorial waters, avoiding a fleet vs fleet action.

The Argentine navy were not able to dispute the British domination and control of the waters around the islands, even though it was able to operate as a "Fleet in Being" (a naval force smaller than that of the enemy, not ideal for initiating a naval combat but big enough to constitute a threat).

It also did not possess sufficient resources to be able to counter the nuclear-powered submarines. Therefore, there was nothing to do other than to go back to port. This was not to say that the war, and even less so the anti-submarine war, had finished for the Argentine Navy.

With the certainty that there was at least one enemy nuclear-powered submarine operating close to the mainland, the Naval Aviation Command (*Comando de la Aviación Naval Argentina*, COAN) ordered the Second Helicopter Naval Air Squadron to patrol in a triangle with its base in Viedma and the radials at 070° and 200° out to 100 nautical miles. In other words, the available resources were maximised to try to locate the CERTSUB that had been detected on the 6th.

This operation was coordinated with the First Destroyer Division and took place between 22 and 28 May, carried out by the now three available helicopters which were each armed with two Mk 44 torpedoes (along with some sorties armed with depth charges). The aim of this operation was to harass the enemy submarine as well as clear the area close to the coast to enable the safe passage of friendly units, be they warships or logistic ships. These sorties were carried out using active anti-submarine tactics with the aim of demonstrating to the enemy that there was a threat above their heads whilst limiting their capacity to operate. Although they achieved several contacts (the strongest of which was classified as a POSSUB Confidence 2, in the afternoon of 27 May), no actual attacks were carried out on them.

This operation was interrupted on the 28th when the command ordered the Sea Kings to return to Espora to plan and prepare one of the most daring rescue missions in its history: to evacuate the personnel of the Calderón Naval Air Station (located at Pebble Island/Isla Borbón) from under the nose of the British Task Force.

For its part, the Anti-Submarine Naval Air Squadron, even though it continued to mount occasional sorties to harass the enemy submarines, changed its focus to one of surface search and carried out these missions in an intense manner. To that end, two Embraer EMB-111 Bandeirante "Patrulha" (on loan from the Brazilian Air Force) were added to its inventory of aircraft operating from the Naval Air Station at Rio Gallegos until the end of the conflict. They also had some help from the aircraft carrier escort ships. Indeed, contrary to what is believed and repeated by many, Argentine naval vessels, except for *25 de Mayo*, did not remain idle in port but joined in with the search, inside territorial waters. Although they picked up occasional radar and ESM contacts, they were unable to locate any British submarines in their patrol areas.

Oddly enough, it was the Argentine Air Force (and not the Navy) that almost sank a British nuclear submarine later in the war. On 23 May, a flight of Dagger fighter bombers returning to San Julian air base (after a mission without finding targets) jettisoned its bombs in the middle of the South Atlantic Ocean. And, by pure chance, almost sank HMS *Valiant*!

> Shortly after 1815z on 23 May a number of explosions were heard, getting progressively closer, the fifth (and last) one being loud enough to shake the submarine (and her Ship´s Company) considerably, and it was briefly thought that *Valiant* had unaccountably become the object of an attack…It was later learned that some bombs used by the Argentines had a short delay in their fuzing, which coupled with the channelling effect of the shallow water would explain the heaviness of some of the detonations felt. (Commander T M Le Marchand, Commanding Officer HMS *Valiant*)

A Job Well-Done

It is possible to compare anti-submarine warfare to a high-risk game of poker, in which it is essential to have a good hand of cards as well as knowing the strategy and psychology of the opponent. This is different to land based warfare where enemy units can be relatively easily identified in advance and is more comparable to a game of chess.

Generally, the submarine, even more so nuclear-powered ones, have the advantage as their sensors are much more effective. The most tangible example of this from the conflict was the sinking of the cruiser *General Belgrano* which, lacking in an effective anti-submarine protection was easy prey for the submerged hunter.

25 de Mayo and other ships of the Argentine Navy, despite being stalked and sought by the submarines *HMS Splendid* and *HMS Spartan*, could not be sunk. Various factors came together to prevent the sinking of any further ships of the Argentine surface fleet.

In the first place, as mentioned before, the British always followed their self-imposed rules and did not attack any targets located within the Argentine twelve-mile territorial waters. However, this was not the only factor. Outside the twelve-mile limit, where the Argentine fleet also operated, no other attacks had taken place as the submarines lacked the freedom of action to reach an attack position.

It is an objective fact that the war was lost by the Argentines and their fleet did not return to risk itself in a surface action after 10 May. It is also a fact that a fundamental cause of the defeat was the performance of the British submarines. However, within the framework of a lost war, it is worth highlighting the operations carried out to protect *25 de*

An A-4Q Skyhawk parked on the carrier ARA *25 de Mayo.* (*Armada Argentina*)

HMS *Penelope* and submarine HMS *Valiant*. July 1982, West of the Falklands/Malvinas Islands. (MoD)

Mayo, that concluded satisfactorily in the face of the threat posed by the British submarines. The aircraft carrier arrived back at port, able to fight another day. That this day never came does not at all diminish the value of the operations carried out during those days in May.

The greatest merit does not lie in the machines, but with the men of the Argentine Navy – the officers, NCOs and sailors who made a huge effort in the anti-submarine war. They are the ones that carried out their duty, in many cases with ancient equipment and with few spares, adapting doctrines in force at the time as they went when facing the threat posed by a nuclear-powered hunter-killer.

That another sinking did not occur is down to the merit of the anti-submarine operations carried out by these men. These operations were carried out well, and for this reason *25 de Mayo* survived. The British submarines did not sink any of the ships of this Task Force for the simple reason that they "could not" and not, as they would like you to believe, they "did not want to".

Of course, it can be pointed out that more could have been done if the nuclear-powered submarines had not been so feared by the leadership of the Argentine Navy. This even surprised the British, as expressed by Commander Lane-Nott: "What we didn't know was the total fear of nuclear submarines that the Argentines had. They created an environment much more dramatic than it was in reality."

However, the Argentine Navy possessed the means – albeit always scarce – experience and motivated crews (in ships and aircraft) even though there was a lack of doctrine to employ against nuclear-powered submarines. Maybe this was not in the conscience of *Almirantes* Anaya (Chief of the Navy), Lombardo (Chief of Naval Operations) and Allara, although it might have been in those of the commanders on the front line like *Capitán de Navío* Sarcona (commander of the aircraft carrier) who had seen the capabilities of the anti-submarine forces from close by. It was of course in the consciences of his sailors and aviators specialised in anti-submarine warfare.

Each sortie flown had degraded the capacity of the British submarines to operate with impunity. The submarines would have detected the torpedoes, and the bombs; when the sonobuoys hit the surface of the sea, the blades of the helicopters and the low passes of the aircraft searching for them; registered the radar emissions and would have known that all of this was being carried out to find and destroy them.

By having just been there, harassing the submerged threat implies winning the battle. In the anti-submarine war what is really the most important thing is the protection of ones' own units.

The sinking of an enemy submarine is really nothing more than a bonus.

BIBLIOGRAPHY

Books/Articles

Amendolara, Alejandro J, "¡Hundan el Portaaviones!", *Boletín del Centro Naval* (May/August 2007), pp. 235-240.

Castro, Fox Rodolfo, *Yo fui piloto aviador naval* (Buenos Aires: Serie Aeronaval, 2005).

Clancy, Tom, *Tormenta roja*, (Buenos Aires: Emecé Editores, 1988).

Craig, Chris, *Call for Fire* (London: John Murray,1995).

Friedman, Norman, *The Naval Institute Guide to World Naval Weapon Systems 1991/92,* (Annapolis: Naval Institute Press, 1992)

Fuchida, Mitsuo, and Okumiya, Masatake, *Midway, la Batalla que condenó a Japón, la Historia según la Armada Japonesa*, (Buenos Aires: Instituto de Publicaciones Navales, 2002).

Hughes, Wayne (Jr), *Tácticas de flota y del combate costero* (Buenos Aires: Instituto de Publicaciones Navales, 2001)

Imperial War Museum, *Lane-Nott, Roger – IWM Interview*, catalogue number 17274.

Jinks, James, and Hennessy, Peter, *The Silent Deep. The Royal Navy Submarine Service Since 1945* (London: Penguin Books, 2015).

Martini, Héctor A, *Historia de la Aviación Naval Argentina, Tomo III*, (Buenos Aires: Instituto Aeronaval, 1992).

Mayorga, Horacio A, *No vencidos* (Buenos Aires: Planeta, 1998).

Pertusio, Roberto L, *Submarinos. Su historia, relatos y curiosidades* (Buenos Aires: Instituto de Publicaciones Navales, 1995.

Powis, Jonathan, "Falklands Memories" *The Submarine Review*, (January 2008), pp. 59-70.

Ring, Jim, *We Come Unseen. The Untold Story of Britain's Cold War Submariners* (London: John Murray Ed, 2001).

Rossiter, Mike, *Sink the Belgrano* (London: Corgi Books, 2007).

Sontag, Sherry and Drew, Christopher, *Blind Man's Bluff. The Untold Story of Cold War Submarine Espionage* (London: Arrow Books, 2000).

Ward, Nigel, *Sea Harrier over the Falklands* (London: Orion Books, 1993).

Woodward, John F, *One Hundred Days* (Annapolis, Naval Institute Press, 1992).

Official records

British

ARA *25 de Mayo* (DEFE 31/233)

Dispatch by Admiral Sir John Fieldhouse, G.C.B., G.B.E., Commander of the Task Force Operations in the South Atlantic: April to June 1982, London Gazette, 13 December 1982.

Operation Corporate – Lessons Learned, Anti Submarine Warfare (DEFE 69/1086).

Presence of Soviet shipping in area of Falkland Islands (FCO 7/4507).

Report of Proceedings, Flag Officer Submarines (DEFE 69/846).

HMS *Antrim*, Report of Proceedings (Naval Service FOI Coordination Cell – request 13-03-2006-172157-025).

HMS *Conqueror*, Report of Proceedings (Naval Service FOI Coordination Cell – request 08-07-2010-112201-003).

HMS *Invincible* Falklands Islands Campaign Diary (DEFE 69/844).

HMS *Onyx*, Report of Proceedings.

HMS *Spartan*, Report of Proceedings (Naval Service FOI Coordination Cell – requests 16-09-2008-071600-002 and 25-07-2011-105719-003).

HMS *Splendid*, Report of Proceedings (Naval Service FOI Coordination Cell – requests 16-09-2008-071600-002 and 25-07-2011-105719-003).

HMS *Valiant*, Report of Proceedings (Naval Service FOI Coordination Cell – request 10-12-2010-101254-002).
HMS *Invincible* ship log (ADM 53/189407); HMS *Hermes* ship log (ADM 53/189351).
HMS *Splendid* control room log (ADM 173/32524, 5 and 6).
HMS *Spartan* control room log (ADM 173/32512, 3 and 4).
HMS *Onyx* control room log (ADM 173/32377, 8 and 9).

Argentine

Barro, Norberto Ignacio – *Armada Argentina* – Commander's Report *2da. Escuadrilla Aeronaval de Helicópteros.*
Miqueleiz, Alberto Raúl – *Armada Argentina* – Commander's Report Destroyer (D27) ARA *Py.*
Molina Pico, Enrique E. – *Armada Argentina* – Commander's Report Destroyer (D1) ARA *Hércules.*
Pérez Roca, Julio H. – *Armada Argentina* – Commander's Report *Escuadrilla Aeronaval de Exploración.*
Sarcona, José J. – *Armada Argentina* – Commander's Report Aircraft Carrier (V2) ARA *25 de Mayo.*
Skare, Héctor A. – *Armada Argentina* – Commander's Report *Escuadrilla Aeronaval Antisubmarina.*
Tejo, José Luis – *Armada Argentina* – Commander's Report Destroyer (D2) ARA *Santísima Trinidad.*

NOTES

Chapter 1

1 Imperial War Museum, Lane-Nott, Roger – IWM Interview, catalog number 17274.
2 Minutes and papers 1-23 (CAB 148-211).
3 MoD (UK). Key documents concerning the sinking of the BELGRANO. Released in support of the Official History of the Falklands Campaign.

Chapter 4

1 Núñez Padín, Jorge F. *Serie Aeronaval 4. SH-3D Sea King,* (Buenos Aires, Instituto Aeronaval, 1993), pp. 5-9.

Chapter 5

1 Email from Andy Johnson (HMS Onyx CO), 3 July 2013.
2 HMS Conqueror, Report of Proceedings.
3 MoD, Honours and Awards – Falklands Campaign, London Gazette, 11 October 1982.

Chapter 6

1 Imperial War Museum, Lane-Nott, Roger – IWM Interview, catalogue number 17274.
2 https://www.cryptomuseum.com/manuf/crypto/index.htm.
3 National Photographic Interpretation Center (USA). *Monthly Index. Photographic Exploitation Products May & June 1982.* CIA Crest Database.
4 Day, D "The Lion and the Vortex", *The Space Review,* http://www.thespacereview.com/article/2258/1.

Chapter 7

1 Bóveda, Jorge Rafael, "El secreto del ARA Salta" *Todo es Historia magazine,* (April 2002).
2 Amato, Alberto, "*Malvinas: submarinos ingleses y misiones secretas en Santa Cruz*" Clarín Newspaper, (17 June 2007).
3 Sontag, Sherry and Drew, Christopher, *Blind Man's Bluff. The Untold Story of Cold War Submarine Espionage* (London: Arrow Books, 2000).
4 Central Intelligence Agency, *Soviet Naval Activity Outside Home Waters During 1982,* July 1983. CIA Crest Database.
5 Barker, Geoffrey "The Mystery Boats", *Australian Financial Review,* (28 November 2003).
6 HMS *Splendid,* Report of Proceedings.

Chapter 8

1 HMS *Splendid,* Report of Proceedings.
2 Fuerza Aérea Argentina – Dirección de Estudios Históricos, *Flight Report and Crew Debrief TC-78 and TC-43,* 6 and 7 May 1982.

Chapter 9

1 Clarke, Martin *Falklands Memories,* at www.upperiscope.com.au (August 2008).
2 Sciaroni, Mariano with Gillis, Matthew "Almost Successful: ARA San Luis war patrol", *Submarine Almanac 2008,* (Texas; Deep Domain, 2007), pp. 25-26.
3 Faccin, Eugenio L. and Speroni, José L."El Bouchard y el fracaso de la operación británica Mikado", *Boletín del Centro Naval,* (Buenos Aires, number 823).

ABOUT THE AUTHOR

Mariano Sciaroni graduated as a lawyer and currently works as a specialist in insurance and commercial law. He also lecturers in procedural law in the law faculty of the Universidad Catolica Argentina. In addition, he has a Master's Degree in Strategy and Geopolitics and a postgraduate course in Contemporary Military History, both from the Argentine Army's Military Academy. He has written two books and has also had many articles about military history published in Argentina, the United States, Germany and Russia and is a member of the Argentine Institute of Military History. He is a Sub-Lieutenant in the Argentine Army Reserve. Mr. Sciaroni lives with his wife and three children in Buenos Aires, Argentina.